Book Lovers on *Why Books Still Matter*

"It's hard to imagine a more powerful tribute to [Joyce Meskis's] life. Readers who want to honor Joyce Meskis, or who simply are passionate themselves about books and reading, will luxuriate in this essay collection."—*Publishers Weekly BookLife*

"*Why Books Still Matter* is a paean to bookstores and their readers, written by wise industry leaders who are brilliant business people, know that words and ideas are powerful and community dialogue can change the world, and have courageously supported freedom of expression in their own cities. It will deepen any book lover's devotion to the power of words and books."—Gayle Shanks, Founder & Co-Owner, Changing Hands Bookstores

"Believing that booksellers were bound to their own version of the Hippocratic oath—as fierce protectors of the First Amendment—Joyce Meskis was a superhero for the reading community. Her legacy blazes on in all of us who are determined to read widely and freely—and in the pages of this remarkable book."—Gayatri Patnaik, Director of Beacon Press

"At a time when books, authors, and publishing are under attack, it is critically important that we remember and defend their importance. This expertly curated collection reminds us that books can connect us, inspire us, and challenge us like no other medium. The rights to write, publish, and read are fundamental to the functioning of our democracy."—Robert B. Barnett, Williams & Connolly, Washington, D.C.

"Joyce Meskis ran Tattered Cover in the time of Peak Bookstores. *Why Books Still Matter* enables us to understand and celebrate those times, as well as the enduring power of books, with a tribute from an all-star team of book industry participants and observers."—Mike Shatzkin, author of *The Book Business: What Everyone Needs to Know*

"*Why Books Still Matter* is a joyous celebration of Joyce Meskis, an icon of independent bookselling, by other luminaries of the book trade. It is a wonderful tribute to one woman and a reminder that principled, stubborn, customer-focused book lovers are the bedrock of a civilized publishing business and a democratic society."—Clive Priddle, Publisher, PublicAffairs

"Joyce Meskis helped make the Rocky Mountain West an area where authors could thrive and booklovers could find a home away from home. She lifted up an entire region, culturally. Read this book to learn how she established one of the country's finest independent bookstores. We all benefited enormously from her extraordinary career as a preeminent bookseller and defender of First Amendment rights."—Helen Thorpe, author of *The Newcomers*

"The title of this excellent collection of essays asserts that *Books Still Matter*, as though that might not always be the case. In fact, what comes across so well is how books adapt. They will always be about the contents. But what is evolving with success is how and where they can be read."—Peter L. W. Osnos, founder of PublicAffairs Books and author of *An Especially Good View: Watching History Happen*

Why Books Still Matter

Why Books Still Matter

Honoring Joyce Meskis:
Essays on the Past, Present, and Future
of Books, Bookselling, and Publishing

Edited by Karl Weber

Rivertowns
B O O K S
IRVINGTON, NEW YORK

Printed in the United States of America · May 2024 · K

Paperback edition ISBN-13: 978-1-953943-30-9
Hardcover edition ISBN-13: 978-1-953943-31-6
Ebook edition ISBN-13: 978-1-953943-32-3

LCCN Imprint Name: Rivertowns Books
Library of Congress Control Number: 2023937763

Rivertowns Books are available from all bookshops, other stores that carry books, and online retailers. Visit our website at www.rivertownsbooks.com. Orders and other correspondence may be addressed to:

Rivertowns Books
240 Locust Lane
Irvington NY 10533
Email: info@rivertownsbooks.com

Contents

Preface:
A Champion of the Book

Karl Weber

L IKE COUNTLESS OTHER BOOK LOVERS and publishing professionals, I was—I am—a devoted admirer of Joyce Meskis. I first heard of her decades ago, when, as a young business book editor at John Wiley & Sons, I was nominated by a colleague to serve on a panel with the topic "How to Launch Your Publishing Career" at the Denver Publishing Institute (DPI).

That chance assignment led to an affiliation with DPI that I continue to cherish to this day. It also took me to the Mile High City for the first time, a visit that of course included a pilgrimage to Joyce's already-renowned Tattered Cover bookstore. I wandered the store for hours, reveling in the store's unique ambience and marveling to realize that a "cow town" 1,778 miles west of New York City was home to what was now my favorite bookstore.

Over the years that followed, I got to know Joyce and to appreciate her many gifts—as a brilliant entrepreneur, a gifted business manager, a creative marketer, and a wise industry leader and spokesperson. Above all, she was a champion of the book: a friend to authors, an advisor to publishers, an advocate for readers, and a courageous defender of freedom of expression. All this as well as a gentle soul with an open mind, a wry sense of humor, and a generous heart.

When we lost Joyce—far too soon—in December 2022, I wanted to do something to honor her memory. My first thought, naturally, was a book. But not a biography of Joyce, interesting as that would be; I thought that Joyce would have preferred to shine a spotlight not on herself but on the world of books, which she served with such intelligence and devotion throughout her life. I decided to compile what scholars call a *Festschrift*—a collection of essays loosely connected by the same general theme, written to honor a beloved and admired colleague.

This book is the result. With the support of members of Joyce's family, I reached out to some of those who knew Joyce well and had valuable insights into topics she cared about deeply: the importance of books and bookstores in our communities and our society; how the business of books and the arts of publishing have evolved; and, perhaps most important, the urgency of defending the freedom to write, read, and publish against those who would limit or suppress it. Two of the essays—including one by Joyce herself—were previously published and have been included here because they provide interesting background information about Joyce and her work with Tattered Cover.

I'm happy to say that all proceeds from the publication of this book will be donated to the American Library Association Office for Intellectual Freedom, which is dedicated to that same essential mission.

Some of the essays include stories about the authors' connections with Joyce and the joy and wisdom they derived from her friendship. Those glimpses are delightful. But I think you'll find that even the essays that don't explicitly mention Joyce are infused with her spirit, and especially her love for books and book people—a love that Joyce did so much to share with the world.

Irvington, New York
May 2024

PART ONE

The Ideal Bookseller

I.

The Tattered Cover: A Lion in Sheep's Clothing

David Emblidge

After a childhood well spent in Buffalo, New York and on Ontario's Lake Erie shore, David Emblidge became a literary wag at St. Lawrence University. He went on to cut his journalistic teeth as an Associated Press reporter and later produced essays (personal and scholarly) and journalism about cultural- and adventure travel, history, food, rock music, and literature.

He spent ten rewarding years as a professor following on degrees in English (University of Virginia) and American Studies (University of Minnesota). A Fulbright grant took him to France for a year at Université de Toulouse; and a grant from the National Endowment for the Humanities enabled him to study with R.W.B. Lewis, Edith Wharton's biographer (Yale University). He also had a bridge year as Director of Development at Edith Wharton's American home, The Mount, in Lenox, Massachusetts.

Emblidge worked in publishing for nearly twenty-five years at Harvard University Press, Cambridge University Press, Continuum, and The Mountaineers Books. He founded Berkshire House Publishers, which was later sold to W. W. Norton. As a book packager, he pro-

duced multi-volume series on various subjects for major trade book publishers such as St. Martin's, Watson-Guptil, and Stackpole.

While on the West Coast, in Seattle, as editor in chief at The Mountaineers Books, he twice taught "Editorial Perspectives on Publishing" at the University of Washington. The publishing company shrank, but his horizons expanded, leading to a tenured position on the East Coast, at Emerson College, in Boston, in the Department of Writing, Literature and Publishing.

In the following essay, Emblidge discusses some of the important cases in which booksellers have played crucial roles in defining and defending the First Amendment right to freedom of expression, including one involving Joyce Meskis and the Tattered Cover bookstore. The same case is described elsewhere in this book, but Emblidge's essay does an especially good job of placing the story in the context of Tattered Cover's business model and Meskis's philosophy of bookselling.

The essay was first published in the Fall, 2010 issue of Media Ethics. *We reprint it here just as it originally appeared.*

"The true profit in bookselling is the social profit; the bottom line, the measure of the impact of the bookshop on the community."

—A. David Schwartz

W E ALL REMEMBER MONICA AND BILL and their clandestine affair in the Oval Office. The Republican-controlled Congress went on a feeding frenzy when they saw an opportunity to attack President Clinton's character for his dalliance with White House intern Monica Lewinsky. The prize they sought was impeachment and its allied publicity. Kenneth Starr became the Special Prosecutor charged with overseeing the witch hunt. Before long, a bookseller was drawn into the fray.

Kramer Books, one of the nation's finest independent bookstores, had sold Monica Lewinsky some books, and Starr wanted to know what they were. Could they be linked to her involvement with Clinton? Kramer Books was threatened with a subpoena for Lewinsky's personal shopping information, but owner Bill Kramer refused to divulge what she had bought in his Washington, D. C. store. Before things came to a head, Starr opted for an alternate strategy—immunity for Lewinsky if she would testify about her entanglement with the president—and in exchange, she provided the details about her purchases from Kramerbooks. That took the bookseller off the hook, but two things had become clear: The bookseller had high principles when the privacy of his customers' shopping choices was concerned, and his resistance demonstrated his commitment to defending the right of free speech (and reading) as guaranteed by the First Amendment to the federal Constitution.

After 9/11 and passage of the USA PATRIOT Act, the George W. Bush White House sanctioned telephone wire taps and Internet searches on many ordinary Americans, bypassing standard procedures that would have required search warrants justified by demonstrations of probable cause. The broad sweep of these activities amounted to fishing expeditions with a huge net. In one egregious case, the FBI tried to secure the book purchasing records of thousands of customers of Amazon.com in Ohio. The FBI claimed that they had bought illegal pornographic videos. Like Kramer Books, Amazon.com resisted. There has been a scattering of other First Amendment cases involving booksellers and libraries around the country, but always touching on the same issue and problem: If law enforcement agencies believe that the public good is threatened in some demonstrable way, then shouldn't they have the right to secure any information that might lead to a prosecution? And, on the other side of the same coin, if the First Amendment protects a citizen's right to free speech, and if that right, over years of judicial decisions, has been interpreted to include the right to privacy about what we read, view or listen to, then why must anyone—a private citizen, a library, a bookstore—turn over information about purchases or borrowings of books, videos, and the like?

Focal Point

In another case, local authorities in Adams County, Colorado, suspected that there were methamphetamine labs producing illicit drugs within their jurisdiction. They focused on a particular alleged operator, Chris Montoya. A search at his mobile home in a trailer park turned up books about building a meth lab as well as an empty book shipping envelope from the Tattered Cover Bookstore, in Denver. The North Metro Drug Task Force commander, Lt. Lori Moriarty, had reason to believe her team was well on its way toward assembling sufficient evidence to start a prosecution, and it seemed to her that securing evidence from the bookseller about the purchase of those meth lab-building books, and maybe other drug-related books, could only help her case. No one argued that methamphetamine labs were a good idea. Justice and the protection of the public welfare appeared to be squarely on Moriarty's side.

That is, until she met Joyce Meskis, owner of the Tattered Cover. The police came to the bookstore, confronted an employee, and demanded Montoya's purchase records. The employee refused to cooperate and took the investigators to Meskis. At that moment, a two-year-long arm wrestling match began--a protracted legal battle climaxing in a landmark Colorado Supreme Court decision concerning the right to privacy of any bookstore customer. Meskis became a local and national hero (she already had high status in the bookselling field), for defending the First Amendment right to free speech—which in this instance meant free, unfettered, private reading.

The bookseller—the Tattered Cover—however also incurred the wrath of those who believed the cops should have this information. In this way (with start-up help from Monica Lewinsky) Joyce Meskis, *local* bookseller, got caught up in the swirl of debate about *national* values and principles. Bookselling is a business, to be sure, but this occupation also can induce a bookseller to become a political philosopher. It can put the bookseller at great legal and financial and even bodily risk, since refusal to honor a subpoena may lead to jail time.

The Tattered Cover Empire

If the independent bookstores in America were arranged in a pyramid of retailing success and customer service or literary programming complexity, Tattered Cover would be at or very near the top. Since 1974 when Joyce Meskis bought the business, there have been various locations and realignments. Each time the direction was "growth." When I met Meskis in June 2008, the Tattered Cover empire consisted of three impressively large stores. The anchor was the historic lower downtown (LoDo) store, a comfortable two-story building with nooks and corners and antique furniture encouraging browsing and the site of many readings, autographings, and literary events throughout the year, boasting a cozy coffee shop and extensive newsstand. The store feels like a large department store devoted entirely to reading.

Under the same name are the Colfax Avenue store, also with 150,000 books, and a smaller, suburban Highlands Ranch store. All three locations are inviting and maintain large inventories, and offer a great deal of service to their communities.

A Bookseller Standing on Principle

It's no surprise that, in 2008, Joyce Meskis became Director of the University of Denver's Summer Publishing Institute. The university recognized that Meskis's reputation as a bookseller and her skills as an administrator would attract top rank teachers to the program. The walls of her office are covered with awards garnered by her bookstores or by her. She has won the (former U. S. Supreme Court Justice) William J. Brennan Award for the Protection of Free Expression; the PEN/Newman Award; the Privacy International Brandeis Award; the American Library Association (ALA) Freedom of Expression Award; the Authors Guild of America Award for Distinguished Service to the Literary Community; and a long list of other honors. Although she is soft-spoken and mild-mannered, with a gentle sense of humor, she is not somebody that the police, or those who want to restrict or censor the public's right to read, should want to lock horns with.

She is a past president of the American Booksellers Association (ABA) and has been an active leader in its Freedom of Expression Foundation. Prior to the day in 2002 when police approached her to demand customer sales records, Meskis had already paid her dues in the battle to protect free speech. In fact, Meskis believes that the never-ending pattern of efforts by one interest group or another to "ban" or discourage the reading and selling of specific titles is a major problem in the free speech area. For example, Tattered Cover, like other bookstores, encountered threatening resistance when it decided to sell Salmon Rushdie's novel *The Satanic Verses* (1988), which offended some conservative Muslims.

The bookstore also took heat from the gun control lobby when it decided to sell copies of *God, Guns & Rock 'N' Roll* (2000), by Ted Nugent, the rock star, which made comments about guns, children, and the Columbine (Colorado) High School shootings that offended survivors and those who favor stricter gun control. Some vocal customers wanted the Tattered Cover to ban the book. They boycotted the store and campaigned against it in the media. There were raw emotions around this issue. Parents, teenagers, teachers, booksellers, newspaper editorial writers all went to the mat. True to form, Joyce Meskis, bookseller, refused to ban the book. She has a personal policy about these radioactive books: She does *not* read them herself.

It's a way to try to stay neutral, to keep herself philosophically distant. But a Tattered Cover manager did read Nugent's book, found some value in it, and concluded that, on some level, Ted Nugent was a good parent. Joyce Meskis believed the protesting parent (the leader of the boycott) had not read the book. So, Tattered Cover gave him one; he read it—and soon cancelled the boycott and picket lines. His wife then brought a critical letter to Nugent at the book signing at the Tattered Cover; a long conversation ensued, and another one later on. The parties may have disagreed, but at least they were talking to one another. This one case illustrates a general point about Tattered Cover's role in the surrounding culture or society: The bookseller is a facilitator of community dialogue, not a final arbiter about what anyone should believe. And yet, fostering dialogue—in lieu of unproductive confrontation—represents advocacy of a "position" in itself, the position being forbearance.

Joyce Meskis wants to be sensitive to the objections of those who complain; she recognizes that we are in a complex society and we don't all think alike. "But, the store should be open minded to the needs of *all* customers." Meskis cited a quick, perhaps obvious example: She is glad to stock books by both (Republican) Newt Gingrich and (Democrat) Hillary Clinton. Not all booksellers operate with such an open mind.

To those who believe a bookstore should stock items selectively, screening out controversial viewpoints or potentially inflammatory material, Meskis replies that she holds a "deep respect for the police, but First Amendment rights trump everything." And, "By offering [a] diversity of materials and author events *without prejudice* [her italics], we are protecting the rights of each one of us. *Without prejudice* means that we do not let our own personal bias against an author's work, or the bias of any individual or group, affect a decision as to whether we stock a book or host a signing. We have had pressure come in many forms, from financial boycott to the threat of physical harm as was the case with the publication of Salmon Rushdie's book some years ago. Yet we cannot abrogate our responsibility to the First Amendment, which we believe to be the cornerstone of our democratic tradition and of our bookstore."

Meskis, however, is not a Pollyanna or a moral relativist. She does not think that all ideas are of equal value. Some ideas, she knows, are positively harmful. "We understand that words and ideas can be powerful. We also know that in varying degrees they can edify, inform, insult, or incur the wrath of the reader. But the cure for a bad idea is not to censor it, because in so doing, it will never go away. The cure is to speak about it, debate it, and gain strength in the wisdom that comes out of the discussion." (Meskis, "To Our Customers: A Statement and a Promise")

The Legal Knot

Lt. Moriarty had a warrant issued that she thought would suffice to force the bookseller to open its records concerning the suspect, Montoya. But Tattered Cover's Joyce Meskis and her team of attorneys took swift action to resist the "invasion" by seeking a restraining order. "Although many people aren't aware of it, in the eyes of the law buying a book is different from buying a bicycle or a pack of cigarettes. Through the years, the protections accorded materials covered by the First Amendment, such as books and newspapers, have evolved to protect the institutions that provide those materials as well." Still, the police thought their case should move forward expeditiously. Everything pointed to Montoya's culpability and for the other suspects connected to him.

A key piece of this evidence was an "empty Tattered Cover shipping envelope addressed to one of the suspects [found] in an outside trashcan, and two nearly new books, *Advanced Techniques of Clandestine Psychedelic and Amphetamine Manufacture*, by Uncle Fester [pseud.], and *The Construction and Operation of Clandestine Drug Laboratories*, by Jack B. Nimble [pseud.] inside the trailer." Presumably these books were purchased by Montoya, and sales records at the bookstore would prove it, or so the police believed.

Legal challenges on both sides proceeded as if in a hard fought chess match. In spite of the legal costs, Meskis never wavered from her principles. Luckily, some financial support for the store's legal battle came from outside as the case escalated from county court to state court, from the lower levels to the Colorado Supreme Court. Two years later, in April 2002, the Colorado Supreme Court handed down its decision. The ruling—the first of its kind to reach this high a level in the judicial system—went well beyond the specifics of the Tattered Cover case. Justice Bender wrote:

We recognize that both the United States and Colorado constitutions protect an individual's fundamental right to purchase books anonymously, free from governmental interference. Bookstores are places where a citizen can explore ideas, receive information, and discover the myriad perspectives on every topic imaginable. When a person buys a book at a bookstore, he engages in activity protected by the First Amendment because he is exercising his right to read and receive ideas and information.

In its own commentary on the court's ruling, Tattered Cover noted, "the Court further held that in the future, anytime the government seeks to obtain such records, the bookstore must be afforded a due process hearing in advance where a court will determine whether law enforcement officials have a sufficiently compelling need for the information." The operative word here was "compelling." Justice Bender also wrote, "Anonymity is a shield from the tyranny of the majority. It thus exemplifies the purpose behind the Bill of Rights, and of the First Amendment in particular: to protect unpopular individuals from retaliation—and their ideas from suppression—at the hand of an intolerant society."

Through all the legal wrangling, the question of what books Montoya might actually have purchased at the Tattered Cover remained unanswered. Joyce Meskis just would not say. But when the dust settled, when the court's decision was finally handed down, and when a documentary film about the legal battle had been released, then there was a public event for an airing of views. Joyce Meskis and Lt. Moriarty were both in attendance, and, finally, the secret was revealed. What was the allegedly incriminating book all about? Building a meth lab? Hardly. Instead, it "was about Japanese calligraphy—it was not, as police had suspected, a 'how-to' manual for making methamphetamine." The police responded to the embarrassing revelation by saying that they need to pursue any and all evidence; the bookstore's supporters liked a different interpretation—that the police had simply been barking up the wrong tree.

> [Tattered Cover attorney] Recht noted that Meskis could easily have disclosed that information to police because it didn't incriminate Montoya—who since has been convicted on an unrelated drug charge. Instead, he said, "she did the right thing and fought the case independent of what book was being sought." "For us, it was always about the constitutional issue," Meskis added. Moriarty said she still would pursue the purchasing records if she had to investigate the case all over

again."As passionate as Joyce Meskis is about protecting the First Amendment, we're as passionate about protecting the community," she said.

And so the debate ended right where it had started. The Tattered Cover and Joyce Meskis had won the arm wrestling match and through the courts had helped to establish a clearer definition of a book purchaser's right to privacy and a bookseller's obligation to protect that right (now police or the courts, in Colorado, anyway, must show a compelling need for the suspected information) but the "authorities" would continue to argue that those protecting "the public good" should somehow, nonetheless, have the option to pry open the doors on an individual's privacy.

The Tattered Cover as Beacon

The Tattered Cover represents an arbitration of taste. With room for approximately 150,000 titles, this bookseller can afford to stock many books on a given subject of varying quality and distinctly different viewpoints (or books written in different voices or styles). The reader can decide for himself what is important, valuable, or respectable; or, conversely, what is trivial, valueless, or unworthy of respect (perhaps offensive or even dangerous). The bookseller posits a philosophical and political position characterized by radical curiosity and freedom, but the bookstore does not try to prescribe what any customer should do with this freedom to buy and read anything he wants. Meskis says "we will never proselytize nor will we ever censor any reading matter that you may seek." (Meskis, "To Our Customers: A Statement and a Promise")

This idea of radical openness unnerves some customers and some other arbiters of taste and has led the Tattered Cover into conflicts other booksellers would just as soon avoid. But Tattered Cover is well prepared. Meskis conducts extensive interviews with all new prospective hires, including questions about attitudes toward censorship and First Amendment issues. "What will push your buttons?" is what Meskis wants to know about anyone proposing to work for her. She tests *all* staff, including backroom people, not just book buyers and salespeople. Joyce Meskis is prepared, herself, to go to the barricades when necessary. A gentle lady she is, but a lion in sheep's clothing as well. At the end of the day, no book, even a guide to writing calligraphy, is an innocuous purchase at the Tattered Cover.

2.

The Saga of a Superstore

Matthew Miller

Matthew Miller, a graduate of The American University and former preschool teacher, began work alongside Joyce Meskis at Tattered Cover Book Store in 1978, performing various roles during his tenure, including children's book buyer, bargain book buyer, store manager, general manager, chief operating officer, and bookseller (his foremost role), until his retirement in 2020. Over the years, he also represented the store on the boards of the Mountains and Plains Booksellers Association, the American Booksellers Association, and the American Booksellers Foundation for Free Expression.

> What can we see, read, acquire but ourselves.
> Take the book my friend, and read your eyes out,
> You will never find there what I find.
>   —Ralph Waldo Emerson

IN DECEMBER OF 1977, I was working as a director of a childcare center, and I wanted to buy Christmas presents for my staff of ten people. I went to a quaint little book shop searching for ten copies of a specific book I had in mind. The book was not in stock in the quantity I needed, but I was told by the clerk that it could be ordered for me and would arrive in just a few days.

When I returned to pick up the books, I was offered not only an unexpected quantity discount but also free gift wrapping for each of the ten books. Feeling that I didn't want to take advantage, I declined, but the salesperson handed me enough gift paper and ribbon to wrap the books myself at home.

That salesperson was Joyce Meskis, and the quaint little book shop was Tattered Cover.

Eight months later, having left childcare to try something new, I walked back into the same book shop where I had received such helpful service and generous treatment and applied for a job. I was about to become a bookseller, and Tattered Cover would be my first and only workplace in that role. I didn't leave until 42 years later.

Little did I know that I had just stepped into the first chapter of a saga about a little book shop in the Midwest that grew into a "super-store." In 1974, the very idea of such an entity was still almost unheard of. To put it in perspective, Barnes and Noble was still a single retail bookstore on Fifth Avenue in New York, though it was declared the "world's biggest bookstore" that year in the Guinness Book of Records. Shortly thereafter, B&N opened a chain of small discount stores and a publishing operation. Borders, too, was just a local independent bookstore in Ann Arbor, Michigan. Even the so-called big box discount stores weren't yet household names. Walmart had only expanded in a handful of Southern states by 1974, and the name Kmart had just been incorporated the year before. The introduction of the first Apple Macintosh computer was still six years away, and the emergence of Amazon was yet seventeen years away. It was a different world than the one we live in today, especially when it comes to bookselling, but the seeds of change were in the process of being sowed.

In recounting the saga of a bookselling superstore, I can only draw upon my own first-hand experiences working for the next four decades with Joyce Meskis—a modest, fiercely determined, public-spirited woman with an exceptional head for business—at her extraordinary bookshop. As I explain the unprecedented metamorphosis of her venture, it's important to note that Tattered Cover never set out to become a superstore and didn't get bigger for the sake of bigness. Though this story may bear similarities to those of other bookstores across the country, it was unique to the time and place in which it existed. Situated in the relatively small Midwestern city of Denver, Colorado, which in the mid-1970s was just beginning to come of age and grow, it was the singular undertaking of its owner, whose excursions to the public library as a young girl had proved formative to her interests, personality, and values. Working hand-in-hand with an exceptional staff of dedicated people, her endeavor earned its success from a responsive community, and Tattered Cover became a champion of the freedom to read—anything, anytime, anywhere—as well as one of the largest, most highly regarded bookstores in the country.

The goal Joyce embraced in building Tattered Cover was simple: to put as many books in the hands of as many people as possible, making published stories and ideas of the ages easily available to anyone who sought them. So how does that happen? How does a modest-sized bookstore provide access to tens of thousands of titles to anyone who walks through the door? After all, when Joyce purchased Tattered Cover in 1974, it was tightly packed into a 950-square-foot space, at the farthest end of the spectrum from being a superstore. In the beginning, Joyce was the sole buyer for the bookstore, carefully selecting as broad a range of titles as the space could hold and shelving them wall to wall, floor to ceiling. She made it a rule from the very beginning that staff members should offer to order any title currently in print if not in stock for any customer who wanted it. This offer was to be made without exception and at no extra charge. As the buyer, she always paid attention to these "special orders" to determine the general interests of the local reading community and continually honed her buying skills to build an inventory that better reflected their wants and needs.

This was just one example of the attention to detail that Joyce brought to every aspect of running the business. As a result, even when Tattered Cover was still very small, the choice of titles was highly regarded for its breadth and relevance by everyone who came to shop there. It was this regard and an appreciation for the comfort provided them while browsing that kept them coming back. Comfortable chairs and floor lamps from local antique shops, hand-picked and distributed generously throughout the store, encouraged people to linger long enough to perhaps discover something unexpected on our shelves. It wasn't long before customers began to visit regularly and make themselves at home while browsing. As a result, sales increased.

Providing the community with its own "sitting room" in which to sample books at their leisure, never being rushed along or frowned upon, soon set the store apart as a desirable place to spend time with friends and family. In this way, Tattered Cover responded to an emotional need that humans have felt for at least as long as modern cities have existed. In 1900, Henry James wrote a short story called "The Great Good Place," in which the main character imagines escaping to a place where he can rest and recover from an overloaded life. In 1989, Ray Oldenburg repurposed the title for his book, *The Great Good Place: Cafes, Coffee Shops, Bookstores, Bars, Hair Salons and Other Hangouts at the Heart of the Community*. That book captured Joyce's insight that creating a place of refuge for customers and thereby fostering enormous community goodwill could be a powerful financial asset for a neighborhood business.

As Tattered Cover's sales grew, the first minor expansions became possible—all the direct consequence of building trust among those who longed to read and acquire books. As the walls were pushed back to house more books, customers flocked in greater numbers to the old

Dutch door, located at the entrance to the original location, in no hurry to leave. The evolution of Tattered Cover had begun.

Thus, the expansion of physical space and the development of business systems at Tattered Cover were organic and responsive to the needs of the community, not driven by any sophisticated business theory or imposed by an outside source. They evolved by trial and error and painstaking financial assessment as we addressed each new challenge thoughtfully, building on existing strengths and holding fast to our founding philosophy.

On a personal level, Joyce's methods were never a function of ambition but rather a natural outgrowth of her instinctive approach to life and how she interacted with the world around her. They reflected what was important to her. That was true in her early years of owning the store and continued many years later. She once described it this way:

I'm a bookseller who still, 50 years after my first bookselling job, gets a thrill out of seeing a person's eyes light up with the joyful and thoughtful pleasure of reading a book. It seems to me the legacy of any bookstore is in the love of reading and the critical thinking fostered in the customers we've served.

This brings me to the heart of Tattered Cover's transformation at a time before superstores were really "a thing": the vital role of providing a marketplace of ideas that enriches a community and nurtures the joy of reading without bias or judgment. All who entered the store were given the freedom and time to explore a vast wealth of books made freely available to them and to do so at a leisurely pace in a welcoming environment.

To achieve that goal, it was important to build a staff of booksellers who were knowledgeable, friendly, well-trained, and could provide a delicate balance of privacy and guidance without communicating haughtiness or impatience—in other words, not going around having their brains on display. Although Tattered Cover basically began as a two-person operation, it was apparent that a team of dedicated people would be needed to move forward. Nine staff members were already there when I came aboard in 1978, and that number burgeoned in subsequent years, ultimately reaching over 300 by the late 1980s. The store's exponential growth from 950 square feet to 40,000 square feet on four floors, including all back-of-the-house operations, was in no small part due to the underlying wisdom, integrity, vision, and inherent business acumen brought to the task by Joyce herself—though, when praised, she always demurred and handed all the credit to a collective effort of the entire staff. She set the example for all in her own interactions and took painstaking measures to see to it that every bookseller she hired was trained to set the same example for others.

To ensure the quality of service she envisioned for the store, Joyce raised hiring and training to a fine art during those years of growth. Initially, this was achieved through an interview process that involved the participation of the entire staff, who then helped in making the hiring decision and in providing on-the-job training to the new employee. In subsequent years, a personnel team was designated to hone the process into an intensive, interesting, often light-hearted, ten-day prep that always preceded a new person's first encounter on the sales floor. This was thought necessary to ensure the high quality and consistency of service to which we held ourselves accountable. Each new staff member was taught the tools of the trade beginning with a personal session led by Joyce, including context regarding the history of the store. Important elements of this training period were based on the core principles and philosophies around which the business had been built: a comprehensive grasp of the inventory, a willingness to "go the extra mile" in providing service, a projection of friendliness and acceptance, and a respect for the diversity of viewpoints. The idea of giving customer service "the Tattered Cover Way" was developed and refined over the years. The basic concepts, such as common courtesy, active listening, and an awareness of the varying and changing needs of each customer, were not complicated. Through discussion, practice, and role playing, each aspect was reinforced, culminating with a self-produced customer service video called the "The Good, The Bad and the Okay" which illustrated those basic ideas.

The training sessions also emphasized an adherence to Joyce's deepest-held convictions regarding the protection of free expression and reader privacy. As a lifelong advocate for free expression, Joyce would often defend the "right to read." In 2002, when the Colorado Supreme Court issued a decision supporting Tattered Cover's right to protect customer privacy and free expression, the store's reputation as an advocate for these rights gained national attention.

During the time when Tattered Cover burgeoned into something so much larger than first imagined—before Amazon was conceived or big-box bookstore chains were established—the store's first modest expansions came incrementally. At first it meant adding only a few hundred square feet by knocking down an adjacent wall. Then, when adjoining space became available, it meant breaking through the ceiling to add a second level, an almost unheard-of concept in this country for independent bookstores, though multistory bookstores already existed in Europe. These expansions were sometimes described as "conservative risk-taking." In this incremental process, the inventory grew, more people came to buy books, more people were hired, sales mushroomed, and a careful decision was made to build out another store, twice the size, in new construction going up in the next block. The original space was then transformed partly into a bargain bookstore and partly into additional office space. The move was facilitated by a large crew of customer volunteers who offered their help in toting cartons of books from the old building to the new one—a remarkable reflection of the love so many people already felt for this community landmark.

As these changes made Tattered Cover even more attractive, the public responded with enthusiasm, and the store's reputation as a mecca for readers filtered beyond our community, into other Western states, and then, as a result of national news coverage, spread nationwide. People came from everywhere, and word of mouth continued to spread. Then, in 1986, a vacant four-story department store nearby became available for lease, raising the possibility of consolidating both stores under one roof. Joyce consulted a team of trusted advisors and carefully examined detailed internal assessments before making the decision to take the leap into a vast new space. This move coincided with the decision to install our first computerized inventory system, making it possible to track sales more efficiently.

Thus, with the steadfast support of the local community, the store once again moved books, this time onto premises that would become known as a superstore of books, independent of any chain bookstore, a move accomplished for the second time with the help of many customer volunteers.

In each case, the decision to go bigger was carefully considered in minute detail, with the potential risks and rewards thoroughly scrutinized. There was nothing rash or overhasty about it. Each step along the way to the store's next transformation was placed as solidly as possible, and each metamorphosis was rewarded by our community of loyal customers. Each time we moved to a new space, they volunteered in droves to help us move the books from one building to another. When asked why they felt such ownership of Tattered Cover, the most common response was access to so many books in a single store staffed by so many kind, helpful people. Perhaps the most powerful tool we had in forging success was word of mouth from one person to another. The value of happy customers talking to friends and relatives about Tattered Cover could never be quantified.

One of the most exciting aspects of bookselling, which became an extra bonus for the local community and one of the surest ways we could bring in new customers, was the rare opportunity to meet authors face to face. Our practice of creating such opportunities at Tattered

Cover began slowly as publishers tentatively began testing the Denver marketplace by scheduling a few authors on national tours with us. Our first book signing occurred in 1977, when revered landscape photographer Ansel Adams came to the store to autograph a new book of his magnificent images, drawing a large crowd. The enthusiastic response by the community to the other authors who followed was reflected in high attendance at events and strong book sales.

Gradually, Tattered Cover developed a sustained partnership with publishers to showcase authors in Denver, and thereafter promotional tours were regularly routed through our store on a more and more frequent basis. As these opportunities multiplied and the store built out bigger spaces, architectural blueprints came to include designated event spaces to accommodate large audiences. An events coordinator was soon hired as part of the marketing department and tasked with organizing and hosting book signings by working closely with publishers through the store's buyers.

These events took innumerable forms. Poetry readings by local authors were regular events. A popular Spirituality Series brought in authors monthly to discuss various views of the spiritual life. The Rocky Mountain Land Series brought in authors to discuss many aspects of nature and issues important to the West. An annual event that always sold out was our Writers Respond to Readers weekend, established to bring a group of highly regarded authors to Denver to engage with participants on a personal level, not just by offering readings and scripted remarks from a podium but by engaging in relaxed conversation over cocktails and during meals. By the time Tattered Cover had grown beyond its first superstore to multiple locations with large retail spaces around the Denver area, we were hosting approximately 500 events per year, sometimes two a day. When large crowds were expected, they were sometimes moved offsite to auditoriums or other large public venues.

By the early 1980s, marketing had become a full-time job on many fronts, staffed by booksellers working on various aspects of promotion under a single marketing director. Team members worked on developing logos and signature graphics, newspaper ads, newsletters, book displays, posters, signage, and more. In later years, digital marketing and social media platforms came to the forefront of our marketing efforts. Presenting the store in a distinctive way was perhaps our first marketing decision—simply creating a homey ambience appointed with antique lamps and overstuffed chairs, as Joyce would describe it, "like a favorite pair of old slippers," and then consistently evoking that same ambience in logos and all the promotional materials we produced. This was integral to our marketing plan from the beginning. Like everything else in Joyce's purview, each element was thoroughly thought through, preferably designed by hand, employing the skills of the artists and writers on staff. Every detail was deliberate, from the choice of type font we used to the design of the logo to the custom color of the carpets—a dark evergreen, soon dubbed by the manufacturer "Tattered Cover green."

While book signings were the largest draw, there were many other ways we sought to engage our community of readers. Non-author events and activities included regular kids' story hours, sometimes including surprise visits from favorite storybook characters. Lavish Harry Potter costume parties were held for each highly anticipated new release, bringing the books alive with elaborate games and entertainments. There were happy hours for readers to meet and mingle, teacher's nights, and special gatherings for businesspeople, librarians, writers, and other interest groups. We held bookmark art contests and writing contests for young readers of all age groups. We sponsored local book drives and public programming, and frequently donated gift cards or stacks of books to show our support to worthy nonprofit organizations in the community. We sent teams of staff members to participate in bike races, marathons, and other community competitions.

One of the most innovative ways we reached out to a new community was by sponsoring a race car at the Bandimere Speedway in the foothills outside Denver. A photo was taken of Joyce at the racetrack sitting and smiling behind the wheel of the hot rod used in the promotion. The car was emblazoned with the logos of some of the standard advertisers—alongside the Tattered Cover logo.

We also "catered books" beyond our walls, providing sales at book fairs, conventions, plays, concerts, lectures, and school events. Probably the first time Tattered Cover ever sold books offsite was in the early years when Joyce and her two young daughters set a up a table at the local Bonfils-Lowenstein Theater on Colfax Avenue to sell books relating to the production during the intermission. Serendipitously, decades later, the historic theater, which had been left idle and deteriorating for a very long time, was purchased by a local developer who wanted to see it preserved and offered it to Joyce to lease and restore as a prospective site for a bookstore. Together they collaborated on a renovation of the almost 27,000-square-foot building, honoring its significance as a Denver landmark. The newly renovated space became one of the Tattered Cover's main locations—a theater of books.

Building on the core philosophy of creating an aesthetic defined by comfortable seating areas and cozy spaces to encourage browsing, eventually augmented by coffee and food services, we were able to provide customers with a refuge, a "great good place" to relax and gather with others. This was the vital element in the evolution of a little bookshop under 1,000 square feet into a renowned independent superstore of 40,000 square feet, employing hundreds of people (themselves book lovers) helping thousands of readers each day find the books they desired. Originated by one passionate reader with a singular vision, Tattered Cover did just that, serving readers young and old, voracious and ambivalent, ordinary and celebrated, all seeking books for innumerable reasons and purposes, and being helped to discover the one or two books they wanted in a vast sea of options.

IN CONTEMPLATING THE STATE of book superstores in 2024, one must acknowledge the changing realities of the book industry and the vicissitudes of the economy. Change is the constant. As Joyce herself put it:

> So, the ideas and challenges abound. Of one thing we at Tattered Cover can be certain, we'll change, and we'll move and, if there is one more person and one more book out there that stands a chance of coming together with our help, we will do our very best to accomplish that end.

Over the last 40 years since the evolution of superstores, there have been remarkable shifts in how books are published and distributed. In 1977, 70 percent of the new books published in the United States were produced by 50 publishers. By 1998, that 70 percent was produced by just five publishers. Since then, the consolidation has continued—yet the numbers of small publishers have expanded, and the volume of self-published books has increased exponentially. Recent estimates of the number of books sold in the United States range between 700 and 900 million per year. The economics of stocking and staffing a very large store have become more difficult. Consequently, many independent bookstores have continued to grow while expanding with smaller formats. New independent bookstores have opened in modest spaces. Even the large chain bookstores have modified their sizes; after years of decreasing sales and reduced locations, some have begun to expand again with more limited square footage.

What does the future hold? Bookstores have always been a low-profit-margin business, and that basic reality will probably not change substantially in the future. The trend to offer a combination of products and services that help increase the bottom line is a more sustainable model. However, new financing models will need to be developed to help sustain independent bookstores and make them viable in the future. Perhaps the value of the bookstore as an essential cultural institution will prompt local or state governments to provide resources to ensure the viability of bookstores in their communities. That may seem unlikely in our current economic and political environment, but who knows when and where the pendulum might swing in the future?

Restricting access to books has also become an increasingly publicized issue. Although bookstores and libraries have always dealt with these censorship efforts, there are currently big headlines about the people and groups advocating for restricted access to books (though those would-be censors represent, in reality, a small minority of Americans). Other organizations, including groups of booksellers, librarians, publishers, and writers, are trying to fight that trend and promote the importance of freedom of expression and diversity of ideas. It will remain an important element of any sized bookstore in the future to be a steadfast advocate for the free access to books and the ideas that lie within those pages. As the historian Barbara Tuchman once put it, in words that Joyce often quoted:

Without books, history is silent, literature dumb, science crippled, thought and speculation at a standstill. Without books, the development of civilization would have been impossible. They are engines of change, windows on the world, and lighthouses erected in the sea of time. They are companions, teachers, magicians, bankers of the treasures of the mind. Books are humanity in print.

The years of pandemic-related isolation renewed the desire for real human interaction, and bookstores can still provide that "great good place" that encourages dialog and authentic discourse. Providing that type of welcoming space will allow bookstores of the future to fulfill that need for human interaction.

The importance of having a literate society has never waned. Recent discoveries about the methods used in the last twenty years to teach children to read have come into question, and reading skills have steadily declined. Bookstores of the future can become even greater advocates for literacy and the importance of reading. Furthermore, bookstores can continue to develop creative activities that attract local communities both within and outside the walls of the store. Listening, and attending to the changing needs and priorities of every community will be essential for bookstores to remain relevant and vital. Whatever form bookstores of the future take, the basics will still apply. Having well-informed, authentic customer relations will remain important to the long-term survival of the business.

In closing, I want to return to Joyce's own words. I believe they summarize the future of bookselling:

Books are the reflection of society as well as its vision. We are "houses of ideas," representing the philosophical heritage, the present, and the future of our society. It's all there for us to pick and choose, whatever our mood—whatever our need—whatever our choice—nowhere else is the choice so great and so personal. Yes, we live a in a technological age where there is instant entertainment. With the touch of a finger, we can bring magic to a screen, but it's not the same kind of magic that the involvement with a book brings. Reading a book allows each one of us to have a very personal involvement with the greatest—and not so great—minds of history, allowing each one of us a chance to bring our own creativity to that interaction— affording us and society the opportunity to build on a good idea, whether it be a better mousetrap, an enhanced computer program, or an improved philosophical ideology.

As library or bookstore, we are the forum for people and ideas to come together.

3.

The Bookseller as Entrepreneur: Joyce Meskis and Her Mission

John Hickenlooper

U.S. Senator John Hickenlooper took an unconventional path to public office. John started out as a geologist, but after being laid off, he considered a variety of career options. Ultimately, he decided to open a restaurant in Lower Downtown (LoDo), a then-neglected warehouse district in Denver. The result was Colorado's first brewpub and a big hit. Over time, he started seven more small businesses and employed hundreds of Coloradans.

After serving on dozens of nonprofit boards and committees, and leading a fight to protect "Mile High "as the official name of the Denver Broncos football stadium, John experienced the power of people working in collaboration, and agreed to run for mayor of Denver. In this, his first campaign, John was elected mayor in an unexpected landslide. As mayor (2003-2011), John worked to expand mass transit, reduce crime, tackle climate change, and improve educational opportunities for Denver students.

In 2010, John ran for governor. During his two terms in office (2014-2019), he helped to move Colorado from ranking 40th in job creation to leading by example as the number one economy in the na-

tion. John brought people together across the aisle and across the state to get things done, from passing pioneering anti-pollution climate change measures and landmark gun safety laws to expanding Medicaid to nearly 400,000 Coloradans.

He was elected to the U.S. Senate in 2020.

I KNEW JOYCE MESKIS before Joyce knew me. Our friendship began sometime in mid-December in 1988. It was several weeks after the opening of my brewpub, the Wynkoop Brewing Company, in the Denver neighborhood known as LoDo. The restaurant had gotten off to a fast start, and we were very busy that evening when one of my staff members came to me and said, "There's someone at table 37 asking if one of the owners is here."

I went over, and there was Joyce Meskis with her two daughters. Joyce introduced herself, but I already knew exactly who she was. Some six years earlier when I'd first moved to Denver, one of my first acquaintances in the city was a woman who worked at the Tattered Cover. We became fast friends—in fact, during my term as mayor of Denver, I officiated at her wedding to another friend of mind, a guy I'd met at the YMCA and played basketball with, who was a producer for the McNeil-Lehrer News Hour on PBS. (That's the way things often happen in Denver, a great city that still has some of the feeling of a small town where everybody seems to know everybody else.)

She introduced me to that wonderful bookstore—already a legendary fixture of the Denver business world—and I became one of its countless customers and fans. I can't even guess how many enjoyable hours I spent browsing its shelves, making literary and intellectual discoveries that would be impossible in a smaller, less-well-curated bookstore. I even became one of the many customers who would pitch in during the busiest days of the holiday season, when the line for free gift wrapping got to be 15 or 20 customers deep. We'd volunteer to go behind the counter and help wrap books following the store's precisely-designed system—carefully removing the price tag, marking it with a check mark to confirm the item had been paid for, folding the edges of the wrapping paper just so, and producing a package any gift giver would be proud to present.

So by that evening when Joyce stopped in at my brewpub, I already knew Joyce's business well, and even had a sense of her meticulous, customer-centric way of managing it. Her life at that time was centered in the Cherry Creek neighborhood, while mine was all in LoDo. But she'd heard about me and my new restaurant, and she'd decided to check us out and to learn what she could about the new kid on the block.

That's how Joyce and I launched what would become a decades-long friendship. And although I didn't know it at the time, that first encounter would encapsulate so much of Joyce's unique and wonderful personality.

The first thing Joyce said when I came over to her table was, "This place doesn't look like what I expected."

"What do you mean?" I asked.

She smiled. "It doesn't look like a professional restaurant designer's vision of what a restaurant should look like. It isn't slick or pretentious. It looks like something someone from the neighborhood would create."

As I was to learn, this was the sort of thing Joyce would say as a high compliment. Her idea of a great business was one that fit into and enhanced the neighborhood it belonged to—not a cookie-cutter template, no matter how artfully designed.

I was pleased by Joyce's comment, of course—though the home-spun look of our place was as much a matter of luck and happenstance as of planning. In our quest for a home in what was then an aging and neglected corner of the city, we'd been lucky enough to discover a beautiful old industrial building with vintage features like a pressed-tin ceiling and post-and-beam construction with old oak columns, 16 inches square with carved paneling. By the time we'd paid for our lease, we didn't have much money left for renovations—so our design philosophy became, by default, "Let's let the building speak for itself."

That's what Joyce noticed—and I was so impressed that she was curious enough to recognize and appreciate the result.

That wasn't the only thing she asked about. We went on to have a lengthy conversation about my business—about why I'd chosen to launch a brewpub, about how we came up with our recipes for beer, and about whether we made all our food from scratch. It happened that I had a partner who was a crazy, crazy chef and insisted on making *everything* from scratch—a detail that Joyce enjoyed learning about and deeply appreciated.

Suffice it to say that Joyce and I really hit it off. We were fellow entrepreneurs with a series of shared interests and values—including, at the top of the list, a sense of mission that provided the foundation for every decision we made in regard to our businesses.

That sense of mission included a deep commitment to customer service. For me, as a restaurateur, that felt pretty essential; unless you provide diners with an experience that delights them, they're unlikely to become regular customers no matter how tasty your food and drinks may be. So when I started the Wynkoop Brewing Company, I adopted the approach to service outlined by the great Danny Meyer in his book *Setting the Table,* built around the concept that the owner of the business must accept the responsibility of *serving* everyone on the staff. I imagine I didn't always live up to that charge as well as I could. But I know I did a better job of running the pub than I would have if I hadn't taken the task seriously in that spirit.

I also wanted to get away from mass market products—the generally bland beers from a handful of giant companies like Anheuser-Busch, Coors, and Miller, which dominated the industry. It wasn't always that way. In 1880, there were 3,000 brewers in the United States.

After Prohibition, thanks to the advent widespread refrigeration, the giant brewers were able to go national and drive the small guys out of business through economies of scale. By the time I opened Wynkoop, we were just the 50th brewer in the country, and one of only about ten or twelve brewpubs. We embraced the emerging brewpub movement as a way to bring back the beauty of craft-made beer, which had once been the norm in America. From the day we opened our doors, we always had at least six styles of beer on offer, all very different from one another (unlike the big brands, which even their loyal drinkers can distinguish by taste less than half the time, as we found in blind taste tests that we conducted). Yes, it costs a little more to make beer in small batches. But we found that what some call the Häagen Dazs principle— that people will pay a little more when they perceive a higher quality— can be applied profitably to beer as well as other product.

I was proud of the service we provided at Wynkoop. But as soon as I got to know Joyce well enough, I knew I needed to learn about her service secrets. She'd famously created a fully-paid two-week training program for every new employee at the Tattered Cover, even those in jobs like cashier or book shelver, which some retailers might consider "unskilled" or even disposable. The two-week program was a big investment in people; bookstores, like all retailers, experience relatively high turnover among their employees. But Joyce insisted that all her team members needed to understand the culture of service that permeated the Tattered Cover. (And of course her intensive training program was one of the factors that helped make her turnover rate lower than at most bookstores.)

So one day, I asked Joyce for a favor. "My company's culture is good, but yours is better," I said. "Is there any way I can sign up to take your two-week training course?"

Joyce laughed and said, "Come and take the first day."

I did. It was a long day, two-thirds of it led by Joyce herself. It began with her saying, "The more books we can put in more people's hands, the better the world will be." She repeated that same slogan two or three times. And I later heard other Tattered Cover managers say the same thing in differing words.

I realized that *that* was Joyce's ultimate mission. The commitment to great service was crucial mainly because that was how her team achieved its goal—to consistently connect people to books that would enrich their lives. Every time a Tattered Cover employee recommended the perfect book, did a bit of research to track down a wayward title, helped a customer figure out the answer to a thorny question, or even wrapped a holiday gift book just right, the connection between Denver readers and the world of books became a little stronger, deeper, and more rewarding—for them and, of course, for the Tattered Cover as well.

Serving that mission demanded remarkable attention to detail. For example, as I recounted in an article about Joyce that attorney Dan Recht and I wrote for the *Denver Post,* every new Tattered Cover employee was instructed, while at a cash register, never to proclaim their love for a book being purchased. While such enthusiasm was encouraged "out in the stacks," at the cash register the next customer waiting in line might be buying a home repair book. They might feel awkward or diminished at the praise the preceding customer was receiving.

Staff training was only one aspect of how Joyce pursued her entrepreneurial mission. The look and feel of her store was another. In 1974, when she'd originally purchased the Tattered Cover, it was a small (950-square-foot), struggling bookstore. Over decades, she expanded and transformed it into what the *New York Times* would call "the best bookstore in America." She hand-picked the antique furniture that gave it a cozy, inviting feel, and she displayed her constantly-growing assortment of books in handsome bookcases (originally crafted by her father), carefully arranged to create private spaces and cozy hideaways.

The same welcoming ambience was preserved even when the 950-square-foot shop was replaced with a 30,000-square-foot space spread over three floors and then an even larger store with five full floors' worth of books. And every time the Tattered Cover moved, customers by the hundreds volunteered—without being asked and certainly without being paid—to help move the hundreds of thousands of books to the new location. Talk about a bond between customers and a business!

The more I learned about Joyce and the Tattered Cover, and the more I learned from her, the more I realized that she was one of Denver's—and Colorado's—great entrepreneurs.

Better still, the time came when I had an opportunity to work directly with Joyce in a partnership to help restore part of one of Denver's most historic neighborhoods.

I've talked about Joyce's mission at the Tattered Cover—to put more books into the hands of people. My sense of entrepreneurial mission was driven in part by my love of historic buildings. Starting in 1976, I'd renovated a couple of historic homes. I love the idea of allowing people to go back and breathe the same air as their ancestors. Having a connection with history is so important—and the beautiful old buildings in many of our center cities are an underutilized and underappreciated asset that needs to be activated and enjoyed.

My business was located in what had been the J.S. Brown Mercantile Building, built in 1899. I remember explaining to Joyce about what the J.S. Brown Mercantile Company did back in the day. This is where manufactured goods would come from the East—cook stoves from Vermont, printed fabrics from England, molasses from the West Indies, honey and corn oil processed in East Coast facilities. They would all arrive on train tracks in the alley. Workers would unload the liquids and put them into giant tanks in the basement and use them to fill one-gallon and five-gallon containers. And all the people who owned general stores would come and buy what they would then sell at retail, making these purchases either from J.S. Brown or the Morey company. (These were the two largest mercantile businesses in Colorado, located just two and a half blocks away from one another.)

As I explained to Joyce, in a funny way, we were still doing the same kind of thing at the Wynkoop Brewing Company—taking huge loads of grain and hops, turning them into beer, and then cooking food and selling it. We were a "mercantile company" of the late 20th century. From this base, we expanded into other activities that took advantage of the same real estate assets. For example, I created a pool hall on the second floor of the Wynkoop building as well as a collection of condominium lofts—just the third loft project in downtown Denver.

Joyce loved what I'd done with the old J.S. Brown Mercantile Building and felt she wanted to create a modern "mercantile company" for books.

The specific opportunity for Joyce and me to partner emerged in part because was worried about her rent going up. New owners were coming to Cherry Creek, and she could see the handwriting on the wall—that she would not be able to stay in her familiar territory. The Tattered Cover was still doing astounding numbers—that wasn't the problem. But Joyce was not in business to accumulate money or to get a bigger house or a nicer car. She drove the same car for years, lived in a beautiful little cottage—maybe 700 square feet—in Cherry Creek, and sent her kids to public schools. But she had a mission. And so she put everything back into the business, and she managed her personal and business finances with the long-term goal of helping the Tattered Cover to grow and serve more people.

The impending cash flow challenges in Cherry Creek would limit her growth potential there. So Joyce approached me to say that she was interested in doing something in LoDo, and she would be open to exploring the possibility of a partnership. This wasn't an idea she undertook lightly. "I've never had a partner before," she told me. And she made it clear that she would never take on a partner in regard to the bookstore, but that she liked the idea of joining forces with a fellow entrepreneur when it came to managing real estate.

We set about exploring options. For sixteen to eighteen weeks, we spent hours every weekend, from the afternoon late into the night, walking lower downtown, talking about real estate and discussing what we admired about particular projects.

Our shared entrepreneurial values were at the heart of those conversations. From the start, we agreed that we did not want to have chain stores, where somebody else had already worked out the business model and all the associated processes. We wanted to have only locally-owned businesses. We also wanted to provide homes for ordinary Denver citizens, not just the wealthiest few.

It might seem odd to some people that two platonic friends of opposite sexes would spend so much time together—talking business. But our common fascination with entrepreneurship and its potential to transform and enrich communities made it feel natural and simply fun for both of us.

It helped that the person Joyce was romantically involved with was an old friend of mine from junior high school, a fellow named Jed Rulon-Miller. In fact, I was the person who introduced the two of them, and when they got married I was lucky enough to preside over the ceremony. I consider our shared, three-way friendship one of the more magical experiences of my life. Everyone knows that Jed was a successful wine merchant (another entrepreneur at heart, just like Joyce and me). Fewer know that Jed and I collaborated on a screenplay about the legendary journalist and short-story writer Damon Runyon. (It's never been produced. Inquiries from film studios may be directed to my office!)

Those weekend conversations about real estate did lead to a very successful project for Joyce and me. We ended up buying a group of buildings known as the Morey Mercantile complex, which we ultimately transformed into what's known as Mercantile Square. Joyce and I mapped out our partnership on terms that were pretty simple: Whatever money either of us would put into a project, we would get back with ten or twelve percent interest, and once that had been paid out we would split the remaining profits. In the end, we agreed to split the profits three to one in favor of Joyce, because she was able to arrange a much bigger loan in support of the project than I could ever have gotten, all thanks to her ownership of the Tattered Cover. It was a very fair and satisfying deal for both parties, and one that we crafted with little involvement by our attorneys—the whole agreement ran no more than four pages.

Most gratifying of all, we were able to develop the complex in line with our entrepreneurial vision, catering to unique local businesses rather than national chain stores. On the residential side, we created ninety apartments, all of which were classified as "affordable housing," not a single "market rate" apartment in the batch.

It was an approach to real estate similar to the one I brought to restaurants and the one Joyce brought to bookselling. We weren't in it to make as much money as we could. We had a mission—to save these historic old buildings and make them the heart of a vibrant new neighborhood, serving thousands of people in new ways.

That partnership with Joyce was both tremendously fun and wonderfully educational for me. I constantly found her endless curiosity and her penetrating insights inspiring and eye-opening. Joyce would talk to anyone about anything, but she especially loved talking about business. And she was a sponge—not just curious, but also smart enough to know what questions to ask and to keep asking them until the answers made sense and she understood the topic from all angles.

I was just one of many people for whom Joyce was an inspiration. I think of my friend Susan Powers, who spent ten years as head of the Denver Urban Renewal Authority, a federally supported, private/public partnership that managed a fund charged with supporting large-scale redevelopment projects in the city. (Today she is a very successful real estate developer in her own right.) Susan says, "If you were a woman entrepreneur in those days, you didn't have many models you could look up to, ask questions of, or learn from. But among those few, Joyce

Meskis was the best, and she became a role model for all of us."

And it would be hard to imagine a better role model for entrepreneurship than Joyce. She combined traits that many might consider incompatible. On the one hand, she was not just an advocate of the culture of service but a consistent practitioner of it. She truly believed in and acted upon the concept that the owner must serve everyone on their staff. Humble on the most profound level, she treated her employees as absolute equals and never made an important business decision until she'd heard an opinion from everyone involved.

But once she had all the information, she never hesitated about making a decision, even in conditions of uncertainty or ambiguity (which of course are all too common, whether in business, politics, or any other field). And once the decision was made, she was relentless and tough in pursuit of her objectives. Her combination of humility with mental toughness was a rare one—and each of these two qualities made the other more effective.

Friendships with Joyce had a way of spreading to form rich connections with many other people. For example, Jed, Joyce, and I became friends with a couple named Rita Derjue and Carle Zimmerman, respectively a water-color painter and an engineer. Rita and Carl owned a couple of little houses in an old, largely abandoned town called Como, about an hour and a half from Denver. Every two or three months, we would all take a couple of days away from the city and stay together in one of those little 600- to 700-square-foot houses with three tiny bedrooms and a cook stove for heat, talking about literature, politics, books, and business. Some of our early conversations about what would become Mercantile Square happened there—and later, once the project was up and running, the discussions just got more detailed and engrossing. Again, Joyce's special qualities as a person were the glue that helped hold these connections together.

I can't discuss what made Joyce Meskis such a unique entrepreneur and bookseller without mentioning her role as a champion of free expression. Other contributors to this book have explored this theme in depth. But as a practicing politician, I want to stress how fundamental the rights of freedom of the press and access to an unlimited range of ideas, opinions, and information are for the workings of a democratic polity.

This is an issue we've seen play out repeatedly in our nation's history. In the Civil War era, when the United States was more bitterly divided than at any other time, the free press played a crucial role—and not always a positive one. Great cities like New York boasted thirty or more daily newspapers, most of them intensely partisan and some of them dedicated to printing bald-faced lies calculated to cast the opposition in the worst possible light. What we today call hate speech was the regular content of their pages, and horrible episodes of injustice and violence like the race-driven Draft Riots of 1863 were among the results. It wasn't easy, but ultimately democracy survived.

Similar periods have recurred since then. During the 1940s and 1950s, after the attack on Pearl Harbor precipitated our entry into World War Two, racial prejudice led to the captivity of thousands of loyal Japanese Americans in internment camps, a terrible blot on our nation's history. The end of the war and the rise of the Cold War rivalry between East and West gave rise to McCarthyism, demands for loyalty oaths, and the blacklisting of writers and others for expressing unorthodox political views. Again, our national commitment to free expression was challenged (you can read some of the eloquent real-time responses by the great *New Yorker* staff writer E.B. White in his collection *On Democracy*). And again, our democratic values ultimately prevailed.

Joyce Meskis and the Tattered Cover played an important role in one of these periods of conflict over free speech. In 2000, five police officers with a search warrant showed up at the bookstore, demanding the purchase history of a drug-dealing suspect. Joyce calmly but firmly refused to comply. Such information was, in her mind, protected under the Constitution.

Joyce and her attorneys defended their actions in court. When the Denver District Court issued a ruling that supported their position only in part, Joyce's team of First Amendment lawyers urged her *not* to appeal it, fearing the risk of an unfavorable outcome that could set a dangerous precedent. Joyce responded, quietly yet firmly, "But the Court's opinion is just not right. We must appeal."

Joyce's judgment proved to be correct. In a stunning precedent-setting decision, the Colorado Supreme Court became the first state Supreme Court in the country to hold that purchasers of books have a constitutional right to privacy. The 2002 ruling stated, in part:

> Bookstores are places where a citizen can explore ideas, receive information, and discover myriad perspectives on every topic imaginable. When a person buys a book at a bookstore, he engages in activity protected by the First Amendment because he is exercising his right to read and receive ideas and information. Any governmental action that interferes with the willingness of customers to purchase books, or booksellers to sell books, thus implicates First Amendment concerns.

In that landmark case, Joyce helped to define and defend the freedom of readers to access ideas of all kinds without having to fear a government watchdog looking over their shoulders. She did so while consistently disavowing the title of "First Amendment Hero." She was simply carrying out in yet another form the noble mission to which she dedicated her life and her work—that of putting powerful books into the hands of readers.

Joyce Meskis represents the best of what booksellers—and entrepreneurs of all kinds—can bring to our communities and to the world we live in. Her passing has been a huge loss—but her example remains an amazing inspiration from which all of us can draw strength.

4.

Heart & Soul—and Mind: Leadership Lessons from a Legendary Bookseller

Richard Howorth

In 1979, Richard Howorth moved back to Oxford, Mississippi, the town he'd grown up in, to open a bookstore with his wife, Lisa. Oxford was home to the University of Mississippi and the great American novelist William Faulkner, yet it was largely known around the country as the site of anti-desegregation riots in the early 1960s. Howorth's hope was that a fine bookstore would embody the humane, generous, and thoughtful side of his home town and offer a welcome to people from around the state and beyond.

Square Books has since become one of the nation's great bookstores and a premier tourist attraction among many in Oxford. Housed in three historic buildings on the town's courthouse square, it includes the two-story main store, with a cafe and balcony on the second floor; Off Square Books with lifestyle sections addressing topics like gardening and cookbooks; Square Books Jr, a children's bookstore; and Rare Square Books, for antiquarian and collectible titles.

A S THE ENTREPRENEURIAL OWNER of Denver's Tattered Cover, Joyce Meskis made that bookstore legendary, playing an important role in the world of U.S. independent booksellers and bookstores and the trade book industry generally.

Over the years, the extraordinary story of Tattered Cover's growth and development, beginning when Joyce purchased the 950 square-foot store in 1974, has been told in various media, including particularly the book industry publications *Publishers Weekly* and *American Bookseller*. The latter publication was issued monthly from 1977 to 1998 by the American Booksellers Association (ABA), the trade association for independent booksellers founded in 1900 which Joyce served as president and board chair beginning in 1990. In this chapter, I'll offer my perspective on Joyce's life and legacy, with a detour or two back to Square Books in Oxford, Mississippi, where I've worked the past 45 years.

Some time after my wife Lisa and I opened our own store, Square Books, I made my own pilgrimage to Tattered Cover, like pretty much everyone in the book business around that time. It may have been around 1989, when the ABA nominating committee chaired by Joyce put my name forward as a candidate for election to the board. Joyce's role in my nomination meant much to me, especially as time went on and I began to know her better, and this fact continues to please me now. Much of whatever we are able to accomplish in life comes as a result of the confidence certain others grant us.

Trade associations exist primarily to enable their members to learn from their peers, and among independent booksellers there was no better model than Joyce Meskis. I had the opportunity to work with and begin to know Joyce while working on the ABA's Publisher Planning Committee, which Joyce chaired. The sixteen members, mostly store owners, of this committee—ABA's largest and many would say most important—met each year with a variety of publishers, including large and small companies, corporate publishers, and technical, specialty, and university presses. We convened mainly in New York, where ABA was then headquartered (later moving to Tarrytown, New York) and where more publishers are based than in any other U.S. city, by far, but sometimes we met elsewhere; for example, a smaller group of us might take a field trip to the headquarters of Ingram Book Company in Nashville, to Andrews McMeel in Kansas City, or to Chronicle Books and City Lights in San Francisco. Our mission was to discuss with our publishing counterparts ways to improve business mutually, always taking care not to run afoul of antitrust law, as our stores are effectively competitors.

Our usual practice was to split up into groups of three or four to discuss a checklist of topics--a given publisher's shipping and packaging practices, its marketing and communication efforts with bookstores, whether its terms and policies were up to date in the *ABA Bookbuyers Handbook*, and so on. Publishers usually leapt at this opportunity to find ways to improve their business and explore some marketing ideas. Of course, they always made sure they mentioned their most important forthcoming titles. Because the committee members represented different types of stores as well as different temperaments and interests as booksellers, we made an ideal sort of general focus group for the publishers. Joyce helped make the meetings effective through her leadership style, which was procedurally relaxed—though we all knew who was in charge—and marked by intelligence, thoroughness, courtesy, patience, and a rock-solid seriousness about books and the business of books. I found her so very impressive.

Years later, I would become ABA president and board chair, and any success I achieved was largely due to Joyce's example. She had an uncanny ability to say little and accomplish much. She could be chairing a meeting with twenty people in the room, and voices would rise and tempers would flare, but Joyce remained calm, letting people have their say. She was poker-faced, unflappable, and when a conversation had run its course or it was time to make a difficult decision, heads ultimately would turn to wherever Joyce was sitting. When this calm, tall, sagacious leader spoke, it was a voice of moderation and clear common sense suggesting a course of action that everyone agreed was proper.

Joyce's stoicism could seem intimidating, like trying to out-stare a cat, although "intimidating" is not proper here as I don't believe she ever would have intended to intimidate someone; indeed, her qualities of being open and gracious invited collaboration. Years ago, when Square Books and the Center for the Study of Southern Culture worked in concert to create the annual Oxford Conference for the Book, I managed to convince Joyce to attend one of these. I think she spoke on censorship, among other topics. While she was here, I wanted to be sure she got to experience something fine and memorable, so I arranged a cocktail hour with two slightly older women I thought might make excellent company: my unmarried aunt, Vasser Bishop, an intelligent, well-read, independent-minded soul, and her best friend, Dorothy Lee Tatum, equally entertaining and gracious, and living in about the nicest old home in Oxford, where they met. I omitted myself from the guest list as I knew these three would enjoy one another plenty without me. For years, Joyce would remind me of this visit, and inquire after Vasser and Dorothy Lee.

And Joyce was no shrinking violet when it came to addressing challenges. When independent counsel Ken Starr, in his investigation of President Bill Clinton, subpoenaed Washington, D.C.'s Kramerbooks in an effort to obtain Monica Lewinsky's book purchase records, Joyce, then serving on the board of the American Booksellers Foundation for Free Expression (ABFFE), played an important role in Kramerbooks' successful defense. "I know a challenge to the First Amendment when I see one," she said, "and I am not going to stand aside and let it happen."[1] Joyce was no newcomer to the issue. She had been instrumental in co-

---

[1] American Bar Association, "Joyce Meskis: Pushing Books and Free Speech," by Chris Finan, September 1, 2000.

founding ABFFE as an independent organization, thereby directing particular focus to its objectives and preventing them from being confused with ABA's many other responsibilities—an example of her clear vision and organizational skill.

Joyce also served as an essential leader when the ABA and its member stores initiated litigation over what we believed were violations of the Patman Robinson Act by particular U.S. publishers. Under the terms of antitrust law, Patman Robinson prohibits some forms of price discrimination. While it is lawful for companies to offer lower prices to some customers than to others, this may not be done arbitrarily; any price discrepancy must be justified by and equivalent to the savings to the manufacturer (in this case, the publisher). After years of high-stakes litigation, the ABA forced the involved publishers to sign a consent decree that they would never violate the act in the future and also to pay the ABA's legal fees. We believed the matter was solved until, in the course of one publisher's acquisition of another, it was found that a publisher had violated the court's decree—a criminal offence. This eventually resulted in a $25 million settlement made to ABA and its member stores—at the time, the largest monetary settlement in a price discrimination case in U.S. history.

I was ABA president during this period, and in the midst of this litigation I sought both to clarify and to strengthen ABA's position in this fairly complex matter by writing a 5,000-word essay, complete with graphs and pie charts, entitled *Independent Bookselling and True Market Expansion*. The intent was to explain how the corporate superstores had not actually expanded the market for books, and, in fact, in addition to causing the closure of many independent bookstores, had caused the market, as well as the number of new book titles and their writers, to diminish—contrary to the publicity spouted by the corporate chains and swallowed by the general press. ABA distributed the essay widely in a staple-bound edition, hoping that reporters and maybe even a judge or two would see this well-substantiated claim. I got a lot of help in researching this piece from a bright, young staff member at ABA named Len Vlahos, who would one day become owner of none other than the Tattered Cover.

Before opening Square Books in the fall of 1979 in my hometown of Oxford, Mississippi, Lisa and I both worked in a bookstore in Washington, D.C.—where Lisa had grown up—beginning in 1977. Located on P Street just off Wisconsin Avenue in Georgetown, the Savile Bookshop had been a local landmark; an article in the *Washington Post* had once written, "What the Library of Congress is to the nation's libraries, the Savile Bookshop is to Washington bookstores." But its luster lately had been dimmed by rival bookstores in the area. The newer, larger Book Annex was two blocks down Wisconsin, and the competition also included Waldenbooks, B Dalton, and particularly Crown Books, a deep discounter advertising bestsellers in every Sunday's *Post* at 40 percent off list price. (Crown Books would later grow into a regional chain that, before long, ended in bankruptcy.)

The Savile had been through recent unsuccessful ownership, and our employer, Wallace Kuralt—brother to CBS's *On the Road* Charles Kuralt—also owned a half-dozen thriving Intimate Bookshops in his native North Carolina, including one in Chapel Hill, which we only recently had departed when Lisa got a master's degree in Library Science at UNC. Wallace made us managers of the Savile the last year the store was open, and we and our ragtag team of booksellers made a valiant effort to save the store.

But it was too little, too late. The store was outmoded. Over time, it had grown into four Georgetown row houses, three of which were on two floors, so that it comprised a warren of rooms and nooks, delightful to many, perhaps especially lovers and shoplifters. But the books were arranged, if this can be believed, not by subject matter but by publisher, with the paperbacks organized not alphabetically by author, but by the publisher's series number. For example, poetry lovers would find books by Denise Levertov, Allen Ginsberg, Frank O'Hara, and Diane Di Prima shelved according to the numeral on their books in the City Lights Pocket Poets series: Levertov's *Here and Now* was #6, Ginsberg's *Kaddish & Other Poems* was #14, O'Hara's *Love Poems* was #19, and Di Prima's *Revolutionary Letters* was #27.

This made for unorthodox browsing for customers—three Allen Ginsberg titles would be in three different places—but it was easy on the bookseller, who only had to look up a requested title in *Books in Print*, find its series number, and go to its publisher's section. It also made it easy for publisher sales representatives to generate re-orders; they merely had to inventory their sections and order what was missing, thus allowing the bookseller to skip this aspect of their job. Nonetheless, the weird system had to go. One of the first things Lisa and I did at the Savile was to reorganize the entire store by subject section, alphabetical by author. Greater browsing and improved sales followed.

But while we felt we were beginning to turn the old Savile ship around, the financial stress on the Intimate Bookstore chain's whole system required downsizing, and the Kuralts chose to close the shop. We had a big sale, emptying out the warehouse of its mostly unsalable books. Lisa made a large sign for the window: "The End of Savilization as We Know It," and we booksellers went our separate ways. Lisa and I went home to Oxford, ready to open our own bookstore having been well-informed by a crash-course learning experience. There is perhaps no better way to understand a business than to work for one that is faltering.

The first hurdle we had to pass was financial. After my fourth visit, improving my presentation each time, with Mr. Cooper at the Bank of Oxford, he finally expressed his willingness to provide a loan of $10,000 to match the $10,000 we had saved. But when he asked me what I had to offer as collateral, uncertain exactly what he might mean, I replied, "Our car?" The 1974 VW Beetle we had bought after marrying was the only property to our name. Apparently it was enough. (We still have it.) With the help of family and friends, we remodeled an upstairs location on the Oxford town square that had been made legendary in William Faulkner's Yoknapatawpha chronicles through such books as *The Sound and the Fury* and *Intruder in the Dust*. Our shop had no street-level visibility, and thus our name, Square Books, in order to help identify our location.

Thanks to gradual but consistent growth, in 1986 we moved to a former drug store building, a larger and much better location. We expanded into a second location just a bit down the street in 1993, calling it Off Square Books, where we began selling used books and remainders, and created an excellent venue for readings. Then we opened a children's bookstore in 2003, named Square Books, Jr, and finally, above the children's store, back where we originally started the business, opened Rare Square Books in 2019.

The third most important expense for a bookstore, after the cost of goods and payroll, is occupancy, or rent. Unfortunately, when a bookstore opens in a place where rent is affordable and then becomes successful, that success generates financial woes. Bookstores are pretty good traffic builders, which means they serve to generate other new businesses nearby. Soon the nearby streets are occupied by restaurants and bars, office spaces, clothing boutiques, and so on, all contributing to increased real estate values and, of course, higher rent. The bookstore is forced to move, primarily because bookstores operate on the suggested retail prices of books as established by the publisher. Technically, a bookseller can raise the price, but few do, or do so successfully. Many large chain operations try to compete by lowering the price (and historically have gone belly-up as a result).

I understood this occupancy expense conundrum both by experience (a key ingredient in the Savile's failure was extraordinarily high rent) and my reading, and I determined from the get-go that, if I succeeded at all, I would endeavor to own whatever property Square Books occupied. True to this plan, we gradually acquired the three buildings we inhabit today. In December 2022 we made our final payment on the third building, which cost, incidentally, eighteen times as much as the first one twenty-five years earlier, which is about the same size.[2]   The three buildings are within about 100 feet of one another. The idea to embark on this general plan was one that I discussed with many of my bookselling colleagues on the ABA board that Joyce chaired—Chuck Robinson of Village Books, Mitchell Kaplan of Books & Books, Barbara Bonds Thomas of Toad Hall, and numerous others.

Community developments contributed to our success. When we opened Square Books, Oxfonian William Faulkner had been dead nearly fifteen years, and there weren't that many writers around—just a few, mostly university professors. But as the bookstore was opening, Bill Ferris came to the university to head the newly established Center for the Study of Southern Culture. Having taught Afro-American studies at Yale, Bill's relationships with Alice Walker, Toni Morrison, Alex Haley, and the poet Etheridge Knight brought them to town for events on the UM campus and book signings at our new store. Also arriving within months of our opening was Willie Morris, who, like Bill, was originally from Mississippi, and who told me he was going to "bring some of my pals to your bookstore." Willie had been the youngest editor ever of America's oldest magazine, *Harper's*, and during his ten years in Oxford he was true to his word.   Before long, we hosted David Halberstam, John Knowles, Peter Matthiessen, and James Dickey, among others.   Novelist Barry Hannah moved to town in 1982, and the first book by Larry Brown, the only writer since Faulkner who was actually from Lafayette County, came out in 1986. Today I estimate about sixty writers to be living here, and we have a steady event schedule that brings over a hundred more to Oxford and our store each year.

The growth of our bookstore led to my decade-long service on the ABA board and my opportunity to observe and learn from the exem-

---

[2] By comparison, consumer inflation generally has "merely" tripled over the same period.

plary leadership style of Joyce Meskis. I eventually found myself apply-ing those lessons in an unexpected way. As an engaged citizen, I ob-served my home town's mayor and board of aldermen struggling to communicate openly, getting crossed up with the local press, and quickly making unanimous decisions in such a way that could only mean some discussions were being held outside the public eye. I doubt I would have noticed this or thought that I either could or should do anything about it, had I not known Joyce and other ABA board booksellers. I threw my hat in the ring for mayor (like another role model, Neal Coonerty of Bookshop Santa Cruz) and was elected by a slim margin over the incumbent, serving four years in our so-called weak mayor system.[3] As I believed Joyce might have done, I worked to establish good relations with the aldermen, and I like to think we took on a good deal and were successful. Four years later, I was elected to another four-year term without opposition. I wonder if I might have ventured this or been at all useful in the job had I not worked with Joyce and others like her at ABA.

The mayor's job was full-time, calling for management growth at the bookstore. Fortunately, this was already under way. Lyn Roberts was already managing, and quite effectively, as she is today. Cody Mor-rison became (and remains) the full-time buyer. A number of other booksellers stepped up under their leadership, and before long our son, Beckett, and his wife, Katelyn O'Brien, were involved in various aspects of running the business.

Many of the matters we tackle at the bookstore are in the political realm. Here in Mississippi, it might be said that there are *many oppor-tunities* to engage similarly, both politically and in operating a business. Here's an example. In 2016 the Mississippi legislature passed HB1523, with its assbackwards appellation, "Protecting Freedom of Conscience

---

[3] A governing system in which the mayor is effectively the CEO of the city but has no vote on the board he or she chairs, except in a rare tie vote.

from Government Discrimination Act," which, according to the Associated Press translation, "allows businesses to refuse LGBTQ people services based on religious beliefs." As a result, numerous local and state governments—including those of California, Vermont, Washington, Minnesota, and Connecticut—banned any government-funded travel to Mississippi. Ninety-five Mississippi writers, including Greg Iles, Kiese Laymon, John Grisham, Ralph Eubanks, and Donna Tartt, signed a letter protesting the bill.

At Square Books, I was immediately compelled to speak up—call it the Meskis reflex—and sat down and wrote, then printed, publicized, distributed and sold (to cover printing costs) a broadside, "All Are Welcome Here," expressing the perspective of our bookstore for the record (see page 60). We continue to distribute this broadside today, eight years later.

While some may perceive this sort of conduct as a risk to one's business, Joyce Meskis was guided by, and helped us understand, the notion that there is greater risk in failing to respond appropriately when the basic principles behind our business are threatened. "Business and politics don't mix," is an adage with a fair amount of truth to it, but bookstores are a different sort of business—different from most other businesses in that the First Amendment is our bedrock, and should we fail to champion it or to defend it, then both writers and readers, our customers, are cheated, and our business is made more vulnerable.

ALL ARE WELCOME HERE

———◇———

Square Books ◇ est. 1979

Oxford ◇ Mississippi

Buddhists, Jews, Christians, Muslims, and atheists
are **welcome** here, as are gay, lesbian, transgender,
and heterosexual people. Republicans, Democrats,
socialists, Marxists, Tea Party members, communists,
unreconstructed Southerners, and Yankees are
welcome here. Our doors are open to men,
women and children, whether Chinese, Japanese,
Native American, European, Mexican, African,
Canadian, Puerto Rican, Caribbean, Russian,
Australian, or Korean, North or South. We do not
care one bit how you wear your trousers, what
color you are, or how you do your hair, even
though sometimes it is difficult not to
find these things **interesting**.

We do not allow guns, cell phone use, or smoking—
indoors or on the balcony. *Yelling* and *running* are
prohibited (except in our children's store, where we
are unwilling and unable to stop it). We do not allow
profanity or other language that may be offensive to
other customers. In spite of what some of our
lawmakers may lead one to think, **people** in
Mississippi are among the nicest, most **hospitable**
people in America. If you are anyone, from anywhere,
we **hope** you will visit us, and we hope you may find
something you would **like to read**. If you do not
find the book you want, we will be **glad**
to get it for you. Thank you for visiting
Square Books and for being who you are.

We appreciate your business and the
opportunity to serve you.

———◇———

REPEAL HB 1523

Over recent years, political differences in our country have increased in hostility and polarity. About six years ago we noticed in the bookstore that someone, perhaps more than one someone, had been routinely turning around the covers of any faced-out books featuring a supposedly Democratic or liberal cause, and turning upside-down the top copy on a stack—a childish but nonetheless annoying act of censorship. This is not the spirit in which Square Books operates. We always have endeavored to represent in our inventory and merchandising strategies the full political spectrum, *to let our customers choose what they wish*. And recently have ensured more determinedly stocking and displaying conservative books.

Over the years, we have held book signings for those from either side of the aisle with books to offer. In 2023, the autobiography of Ron DeSantis, the Florida governor and presidential candidate, was released. DeSantis was a proud supporter of Florida's HB7, the "Individual Freedom Act," which "prevents teachers from discussing advantages or disadvantages based on race," thus shutting off education about "a wide range of topics enshrined by the First Amendment," according to Nadine Johnson of PEN America (March 10, 2023). He was also an advocate of the 2021-22 school year *ban of 565 books* in Florida schools. Soon after his own book was published, DeSantis began claiming that his role in or support for book banning was "a liberal hoax," obviously frightened by the idea that someone *might want to ban his book*, while also clearly tickled that the stunt was creating greater publicity for his book and for him.

No matter. We had a ten-copy stack of DeSantis's book on our front-gondola display. We sold one copy the first week, a few more later.

Across the nation, in controversies involving the First Amendment, one may find independent bookstores at the tip of the spear. Many shall never forget the 1989 publication of Salman Rushdie's *The Satanic Verses*, which led to the bombings of two Berkeley bookstores and bomb threats that blanketed the U.S. and other nations—twenty of which banned the book.[4]   While the major chain stores completely removed the book from display, the vast majority of independent stores did not. At Square Books, after some discussion regarding staff safety, we decided to display it on the front counter of the store, and that no bookseller from our staff who wished not to work behind the counter would be required to do so. Not a single bookseller exercised that option, even when we did get a threat.

Joyce Meskis's lifelong commitment to the First Amendment and her leadership in this particular arena served to prepare booksellers for that moment, and that example now carries on beyond her life. Joyce is now in a better place, writing, thinking, and saying whatever the hell she likes—though I'm certain I never heard her cuss.

---

[4] Rushdie spent years in hiding initially following the fatwa, later somewhat resuming a normal life; as we know, he was nearly killed in an assassination attempt in August, 2022.

5.
"A Black Bookstore and More": Bringing Ideas, Inspiration, and Involvement to an Underserved Community

Clara Villarosa

Clara Villarosa is an entrepreneur, author, and motivational speaker. She was the co-founder of the Hue-Man Experience Bookstores in Denver, Colorado and Harlem, New York, one of the highest earning African-American bookstores in the United States from the 1980s to the 2000s.

In 1994, she was named National Minority Entrepreneur of the Year by the Minority Business Development Agency of the US Department of Commerce. Her book Down to Business: The First 10 Steps to Entrepreneurship for Women *(Penguin, 2009) was nominated for an NAACP Image Award. She earned a bachelor's degree in education and psychology at Roosevelt University and a master's degree in social work from Loyola University.*

A BOOKSTORE IS A BUSINESS. It sells products that need to attract and satisfy consumers, and it must make a profit so that it can stay in business and continue to serve its customers. But a bookstore is also much more than a business. It serves as a community hub where people meet, share ideas, learn, grow, and create important bonds with one another. It helps to drive and shape the community's social, cultural, artistic, political, and intellectual life. It opens doorways to understanding, empathy, creativity, and joy for people of all backgrounds and ages, from the smallest children to the oldest seniors.

A great bookstore serves all these roles. And nowhere is this more true than with a bookstore designed to serve a particular segment of the community that may otherwise be neglected or ignored. That's the story of my bookstore, the Hue-Man Experience, in its two incarnations—first in Denver, Colorado and later in New York City's Harlem.

Like many people in the book business, I am a lifelong reader and book lover who didn't originally intend to make books the center of my life work. Born on Chicago's South Side in 1930, I became a psychotherapist trained in the psychoanalytic method of analyzing and treating people, and I worked at clinics and hospitals with a variety of patients, especially children. I then embarked on a second career as a vice president of human resources at a local bank in Denver. That's where I learned about the basics of business and finance. I also continued to practice psychotherapy part-time.

I was doing all right in my life and work, but I wasn't necessarily excited about my job at the bank. In my fifties, two forces combined to nudge me toward a new career as a bookseller.

One was my then-boyfriend, a man named Louis Freeman. Louis had the desire to become an entrepreneur, and his idea was to start a card shop. It was a pretty good idea, but he had the same problem lots of would-be entrepreneurs have: no money.

The other force was the top management at the bank. I was good at my job, but they weren't happy with me. They didn't have any concrete complaint against me, but I made them uncomfortable because I was what you might call mouthy: I tended to tell people exactly what I thought about things, which was not considered the proper style for someone in a leadership role at a bank.

I knew my communication style rubbed some people at the bank the wrong way. So I wasn't surprised when I got wind of the fact that they wanted to fire me. But they would find that getting rid of me would be easier said than done. I asked for a meeting with my boss, and I told him, "Excuse me! I hear you are interested in terminating me. But you can't terminate me without going through the appropriate progressive disciplinary steps—a first warning, a second warning, and so on." (Remember, I was an HR expert! And all of my performance reviews to that point had been fine.) My boss was dismayed, but he knew I was right.

However, I didn't want to leave him hanging. I went on to say, "It's all right, you don't have to fire me. I will resign. But here's an envelope with a dollar amount written on it. Give me this amount as a severance package, and I'm out the door."

Without divulging the exact number, let's say it was in the five figures—not a huge amount of money, but enough to give me a comfortable transition to my next step. Sensibly, the bank agreed, and we parted on friendly terms.

I took the check home to my boyfriend and informed him, "Guess what, Louis? Your dream is going to come true—in a way. We are going to start a business together. But not a card shop—a bookstore."

Louis was good with that, because he was like me—a lifelong book person. And he also understood, like me, that African Americans are a badly underserved community that needs bookstores to address their reading preferences and needs.

Of course, Black communities across America get short shrift in lots of ways. Health care, government services, schools, even supermarkets are harder to find in African-American neighborhoods than in white ones. But books and bookstores are a special problem. There has long been a myth in the world of publishing that African Americans "don't read." It has never been true. Like all people, Black Americans are hungry for good books, especially ones that relate to their own lives and interests . At that time, mainstream publishers had almost exclusively catered to white readers and issued only a relatively handful of books by and for Black people. Because of the same myth, the big bookstore chains had been slow to open stores in majority Black neighborhoods, and books dealing with topics of interest to Black readers either got stuck on a shelf in a back corner of bookstores or dispersed among thousands of other titles, making them very hard to find.

With such a lack of relevant products and such poor access to those that existed, African-American readers had a very hard time getting their hands on the books they wanted. So sales of Black-focused books had been artificially low, which reinforced the publishers' false belief that Black people just did not read. It was a vicious cycle that I wanted to try to help break.

The first problem I had to address was the fact that I didn't know anything about starting or running a bookstore.

Denver was a good place to be a bookseller—it was a large, growing city with a relatively highly educated population. The African-American community was not huge—I sometimes said, "Denver had five Black people, plus me" (a slight exaggeration). There were already a few Black-owned bookstores in the city. But they were very small and struggling, and when I visited them to say I was thinking of opening a store of my own, the owners understandably viewed me as competition. They weren't interested in offering any advice or help.

That's where Joyce Meskis came into the story.

In 1983, as I was working on planning my bookstore launch, the Tattered Cover was already the most famous bookstore in Denver and one of the most famous in the country. I used to shop there myself. I wasn't crazy about the décor. Tattered Cover had seating areas furnished with old chairs and dim lights to create a homey atmosphere. I wanted something brighter, more modern and professional-looking—closer to what Barnes & Noble was then doing. But like most other people, I was very impressed by the Tattered Cover's customer service and their wide selection of titles. It was obvious that they knew how to run a successful bookstore.

So I called up the owner, Joyce Meskis, and told her about my plan to launch an African-American bookstore in Denver. She immediately offered to help me in any way she could.

That's how my long friendship with Joyce Meskis began.

Joyce invited me to visit her at the Tattered Cover so she could help me get started on my education in bookselling. She gave me a backstage tour of the store and taught me the ropes about inventory management, organizing the product, hiring and training staff—the works. At the time, I had no idea where a bookseller would go to get books, so Joyce explained to me about the role of wholesalers, who can provide one-stop access to titles from a wide range of publishers. "Go to Ingram," she said, naming the world's largest book wholesaler. "They can get you every book you need."

I began to feel as though this crazy idea of starting a bookstore might actually work.

By this time, I'd found another partner—Yvonne Freeman (no relation to Louis)—who was able to provide some additional money to fund our business startup. Between my nest egg and Yvonne's contribution, we now had a total capitalization of $35,000, which was a decent amount to get started with. After a diligent search for an appropriate location, we found a 1,500-square-foot row house at 911 23rd Street, near Denver's historic Five Points District on a street with good foot traffic. What's more, the local office of Ingram's, which we now knew was going to be our chief source of products, was just a mile away. We signed the lease and picked a date in early 1984 for the launch of our store.

We also needed a name for our store. My working experience in human relations provided an inspiration. I woke up one night with a name in my mind—The Hue-Man Experience Bookstore—along with a slogan, "Shades and Colors of Man." Over the years, we would use that slogan along with other taglines, such as "A Black Bookstore and More," to suggest the range and focus of products and topics we would provide.

On February 3, 1984, The Hue-Man Experience Bookstore had its grand opening. My minister had been planning to offer a blessing before the ribbon was cut, but he got stuck in traffic, so a girlfriend of mine who was also a minister provided a suitable prayer. Joyce Meskis was there to offer her good wishes, along with a huge and excited crowd of book lovers. The Hue-Man Experience was officially a Denver hot spot.

Still, turning one day's success into a long-term business strategy took a lot of hard work. In those pre-internet days, just finding African American books from the hundreds of U.S. publishers was a massive job, requiring me and my partners to flip through page after page of all the separate catalogs. Ninety percent of the books we stocked were by African-American authors, but we would also carry books by white authors that dealt with Black-related topics (like African culture or the history of slavery, for instance).

Gradually the major publishers began to channel information and ideas our way. They appreciated the fact that we were a specialty outlet for books and authors that they might otherwise struggle to sell. Over time, we got to know all the publisher's sales reps. They were almost all white—the one Black rep I recall is the late Manie Barron of Random House, who later became publisher of Amistad Press as well as a notable literary agent. But white or Black, the reps would look out for the Black books coming from their companies and send me their seasonal catalog with selected pages turned down for me. That made it easy for me to order the titles I knew my customers would appreciate.

I also made a conscious effort to turn myself into a walking advertisement—not just for the bookstore but for the whole concept of African-American culture, community, and pride. Wherever I went in public, I wore Afro-centric clothing and jewelry (we eventually started selling the jewelry as a side line at the bookstore). People began to recognize Miss Clara as "the Hue-Man Lady." And whenever there was an event in or around Denver that would be of interest to African Americans—a lecture, a concert, an art exhibition—I would call the organizations and ask whether I could come and sell books. I would bring an assortment of titles (of course including any books by an author who might be giving a talk) and set up a table where people could browse and make discoveries. Black people and many others were excited to see such an inspiring range of books by African Americans—books that the mainstream media had led them to believe simply didn't exist.

Over time, we added other elements to our marketing mix. We sponsored a radio program, "Black Montage" hosted on KUVO-FM by Louis Freeman on Sunday mornings. We also published a quarterly newsletter that carried a steady stream of news about books by and for African Americans, read by people around the country. And we developed partnerships with the Cleo Parker Robinson Dance Company, Eulipions Theatre, and other community organizations.

As a result, The Hue-Man Experience became an important thread of African-American life in Denver and the entire state of Colorado. The formula was simple: I supported the community, and the community supported me back. As I wrote in the business plan we shared with people interested in investing in our company:

The value of the Black heritage and the respect for the Black consumer is the driving force of the business. It is what makes the store more than a business and sets it apart from other enterprises. The owners have established not just a business, or bookstore, or Black bookstore, but a business that can be something the Black community can point to with pride and feel a sense of ownership, knowing that the store serves them while still demonstrating the best of good business.

The single biggest factor that put The Hue-Man Experience on the map was the stream of notable authors who visited us to give presentations, meet readers, and autograph books. This was one of the things I'd asked Joyce about: "How can I get the African-American authors to come to my store?"

She said, "Just start doing signings. The authors and publishers will count how many books get sold. The more you sell, the more often they'll want to come."

Her simple strategy worked. The legendary James Baldwin was one of our first guest speakers. Others included Toni Morrison, Terry McMillan, Alice Walker, and Walter Mosley. We supported E. Lynn Harris in his early days; as he wrote in an article in 2001, "She [Clara] took some of my books into her store when I was still selling them from the back of my car. I've never forgotten her for that." Harris went on to become a groundbreaking gay novelist, author of ten consecutive *New York Times* bestsellers prior to his untimely death in 2009. We also hosted appearances by popular celebrities who usually aren't thought of as authors. For example, actress Ruby Dee autographed copies of her memoir, musician Wynton Marsalis read from his writings on jazz, and Alex English, a star with the Denver Nuggets of the NBA, came to promote his three books of poetry. Visits by luminaries like these made The Hue-Man Experience a happening place that ordinary folks wanted to visit regularly.

And of course, events like these sell books—and once that started to happen, the publishers began knocking on my door with regularity. The Hue-Man Experience became a recognized force in the industry, especially where books by African-American authors were involved. By 1995, when General Colin Powell was ready to publicize his memoir (and being widely talked about as a potential presidential candidate), I was one of the first to call Random House and offer my store for a big event during the week of publication. I must have gotten a junior staffer without much experience on the phone, because their initial response was to turn me down. But as I heard later, someone with more knowledge quickly spread the word: "You'd better call Clara Villarosa back fast. Otherwise she'll be calling the president of Random House." (I guess I was still what some people consider mouthy!)

Sure enough, they called me back, and we arranged a gala welcome for General Powell at The Hue-Man Experience. On October 4, 1995, he signed 600 copies of his book at our store, where he was greeted by Denver Mayor Wellington Webb and Governor Roy Romer (wearing his trademark leather jacket). Later that same day, Powell visited the Tattered Cover and signed another 2,100 copies. The *Rocky Mountain News* claimed it was a record for most books signed by an author in a single day. When it came to selling books, Joyce Meskis and I packed a pretty good one-two punch.

My most special relationship with any author was with Maya Angelou. I was a little surprised that she and I became so close; she was a renowned literary figure constantly sought out by celebrities from the arts, culture, and media. Those who knew her best sometimes said to me, "Maya takes to you because you're like her, so down to earth." And my daughter Linda pointed out, "Most of the people around her are younger, but you're her age." Linda felt Maya liked having a peer like me as a friend, since she was surrounded by so many talented young people who were vying to be her protégés.

Whatever the reasons, Maya and I hit it off very well. The first time she invited me to a party at her house in Winston-Salem, North Carolina, I was inclined to turn her down ("I can't do that!"). But my daughters Linda and Alicia insisted I should go: "We are getting you a dress and making you a reservation to stay at the Embassy Suites!"

I gave in, and of course I had a lovely visit with Maya. And after that, she would make me stay with her at her house. I'll always remember experiencing Thanksgiving dinner at Maya's and having her introduce me to Oprah Winfrey by saying, "You know those books I'm always sending you? I get them from *her* store!"

With the help of friends like these, The Hue-Man Experience became a super successful bookstore—first profitable, then growing steadily in size. By 1987, we had to double the size of the store, which had grown to stock almost 5,000 different book titles. Four years later, I was able to buy the building containing the store, which also housed an art gallery and a shop offering Afrocentric products. I started routinely describing The Hue-Man Experience as "the largest African American bookshop in the country." This wasn't based on any hard evidence; I was using the theory, "Name it and claim it," which I find is usually a pretty effective promotional strategy. In reality, I suspect that the Dallas bookstore Black Images, owned by Emma Rogers, may have been larger—after all, Dallas has about four times as many Black people as Denver. But there were times when I even made that claim about being the biggest in front of Emma—and she never contradicted me.

Through it all, I stayed in touch with Joyce Meskis. She was a special person—very quiet, but so generous with her time and insights. I could call her and ask about anything.

Knowing that Joyce was on the board of the American Booksellers Association, I became curious about the organization. When I met with other Black booksellers, I would ask, "Are you a member of the ABA?"

They would usually respond, "No, that's a white organization."

"Really?" I said, "You're not allowed to join the ABA?"

"That's not it, I'm just not interested."

I had a feeling they were missing out on something. So I asked Joyce if I could join the ABA, and she said, "Sure!" I soon decided I was going to create an African-American interest group within the ABA. Emma Rogers from Dallas became a member, along with many of our counterparts from Black-owned bookstores around the country; competition among us was never an issue, because we were each located in a different city that we considered our home territory. The result was a vibrant group that met annually to swap ideas, share news, and attend specialized educational workshops in conjunction with the ABA convention, usually held at the Javits Center in New York City. I became president of this organization as well as an ABA board member in my own right.

The success of The Hue-Man Experience opened many other doors for me. In 1996, I was invited to South Africa on a trade mission with other African-American business owners, looking for opportunities to expand economic partnerships between Black Americans and Africans. One of the places we visited was the Hector Pieterson School in Soweto, named after the first child killed in the Soweto uprising that ultimately led to the end of apartheid. It was a moving experience to meet some of the children who represented the future of South Africa. But as a book industry leader, I was shocked and saddened when they opened a door to a room they called the school library: it contained no books, only a collection of old *National Geographic* magazines. Scant funding from the government was to blame.

I came home determined to do something about this. I used the same methods I'd learned over my years as an entrepreneur and bookseller: I just picked up the phone and started making calls. I asked my fellow African-American booksellers to donate books. I called publishers and asked them to send books of interest to young Black Africans. And as the donations began to roll in, I got the Hellman Shipping Company to deliver them to Johannesburg, all on a pro bono basis.

To make sure the project was successful, I traveled back to South Africa myself. I was there on the dock in Johannesburg when the container filled with 7,000 pounds of books was unloaded and transferred to a truck for delivery to the school. The booksellers and publishers were so excited by the results that, a year later, we conducted another book drive for South Africa and collected another 10,000 pounds of books for local schools.

I've also had the opportunity to serve as a consultant and advisor to many people and organizations interested in making connections with the African American community through the power of books. A couple of typical examples: in 1995, when Candice Brown, a librarian from Littleton, Colorado, was asked to create a library service in the community room of the Sierra Vista apartment complex in Arapahoe County, she discovered that 85 percent of the residents were African Americans. Realizing that, as a white woman, she wasn't sure how to serve this population well, she called on me for advice. In addition to talking with her about some of the great Black authors she needed to know about, I pointed her to the Blackboard List, which focused on bestselling books of interest to Black communities. The same year, I offered similar support to another librarian working to launch book discussion groups for African American inmates in a detention center in Englewood, Colorado.

I enjoyed having chances like these to help spread good news about the richness of Black literature and the eagerness of African-American readers to enjoy and appreciate it. Having these books accessible, as well as having places where Black readers can meet one another and the authors they love, is important for the Black community— which made places like The Hue-Man Experience so essential.

One special audience for whom books are particularly important is children. During my years as a bookseller, I continued to practice psychotherapy part-time, especially with children. I brought some of those experiences to the table in August, 1989, when I wrote an article in *American Bookseller* about the value of children's books by and for African Americans:

Whether they experience reading through libraries, bookstores, or in schools, most African-American children see themselves underrepresented in books. The stories they read are most often about white children and their experiences, cultures, and histories . . . If you are absent or simply blended in, the subliminal message is that you do not exist, which can especially make children feel devalued, unimportant, and insignificant.

I'm happy to say that, in the years since then, the number and quality of children's books featuring Black characters, settings, and themes has continued to grow. This is good not just for Black children but for all young readers. There's nothing like a book to help a child develop empathy, understanding, and openness toward other people. That's why I wrote, in that same article, that "Booksellers can be instrumental in teaching and promoting good race relations." And of course the same philosophy applies to learning respect and acceptance for people across many other potential dividing lines, including gender, ethnicity, language, religion, and sexuality. Those of us in the book business are doing a better job of representing these values than we did in the past—but we can still do much more.

After operating The Hue-Man Experience in Denver for 19 years, I sold the store to three young partners in the early 2000s and then moved to a co-op apartment in New York City. (I'm sorry to say that the store is no longer in business in Denver.) My plan in retiring was just to be a full-time Grandma. But the plan was delayed when I was approached by a group of people from Harlem USA, a federally designed economic empowerment zone then under development. "We need you to open a bookstore in New York," they said.

I guess I must not have been really ready to retire, because I accepted the invitation.

I got two partners to put up the money to launch the store. They were Celeste Johnson and Rita Ewing, the wives of two star players from the New York Knicks basketball team. We opened up a new Hue-Man Experience Bookstore in the epicenter of African-American culture—on 125th Street, near the world-famous Apollo Theater and next door to the Magic Johnson Theater in the Harlem USA Retail Complex.

The store was also just two blocks away from the post-White House office of Bill Clinton. So the former president had a very short walk on June 22, 2004, when he came to The Hue-Man Experience Bookstore in Harlem to celebrate the release of his memoir *My Life.* We sold over 2,000 copies. My goal from the day we opened the doors of Hue-Man in Harlem was to build a bookstore that would generate at least a million dollars in annual revenue—and during the next two years, I accomplished that and more.

Today I have gone back to my original plan in moving to New York—namely, to spend more time being Grandma to my beautiful grandkids. I'm also dabbling in art (my paintings, color-coordinated to match with the furniture, adorn the walls of my co-op apartment), and of course catching up on all the reading I didn't always have time to do as an entrepreneur—mainly fiction and what I think of as "interesting nonfiction." My daughter Linda is a *New York Times* contributing writer, a former senior editor at *Essence,* a professor of journalism, and the author of the book *Under the Skin,* a finalist for the Pulitzer Prize, about the health care disparities suffered by African Americans. Her sister Alicia is a freelance journalist and a Pilates instructor. Both are New Yorkers, which means this is the city where I need to be.

As you can see, I've had an eventful life. Now that I'm retired again—this time for real—I can only hope that the next generation of African-American booksellers will enjoy as much fun and success as I had connecting the richness of our community's literary life to the broader stream of Black American culture.

6.
The Vital Role of the Bookseller in Our Culture and in Our Communities

Carole Horne

Carole Horne started as a bookseller at Harvard Book Store in 1974, beginning a 47-year career. In 1978 she became the store's book buyer, a job she would hold for almost thirty years. As the store grew, she became the head buyer, with responsibility for all the company's book buying, until she became general manager of the company in 2007. In the late 1980s she was on the faculty of the American Booksellers Association's Booksellers School, teaching in the U.S. and in Central Europe. She was active in the bookselling community, serving as President of the New England Booksellers Association in the mid-1990s, on the Board of Directors of the American Booksellers Association in the late 1990s, and as a frequent speaker at regional and national conventions. She retired in June of 2021.

W HEN I CHOSE "The vital role of the bookseller in our culture and in our communities" as my topic for this *Festschrift* honoring Joyce Meskis, it seemed a simple thing to write about. After all, Joyce was such an exemplar of everything a bookseller should be in her community. But the longer I thought about it, the more I realized that we booksellers are involved in not just one community, but in several. The three that stand out to me are the community of booksellers; the community of readers (and the authors whose books they read); and the larger community where a bookstore is located—and beyond. Joyce was a hero in all three.

Because it's what most people think of when they think about the role of the bookstore in the community, I'll start with the community of readers and authors.

In his research, Ryan Raffaelli at Harvard has studied what he calls "The Three Cs"—Community, Curation, and Convening.* He set out to discover how independent bookstores managed to survive and even thrive despite competition from Amazon and other online retailers. His findings show how much consumers still value community and personal contact, and they say a lot about the role of indie bookstores in communities. Raffaelli defines the Three Cs this way:

- o **Community:** Independent booksellers were some of the first business leaders to champion the idea of *localism*. Bookstore owners across the nation promoted the idea of consumers supporting their local communities by shopping at neighborhood businesses. Indie bookstores won customers back from Amazon, Borders, and other big industry players by stressing their strong connection to local community values.

---

* "Reinventing Retail: The Novel Resurgence of Independent Bookstores," by Ryan L. Raffaelli, Working Paper 20-068, Harvard Business School, January 2020, https://www.hbs.edu/ris/Publication%20Files/20-068_c19963e7-506c-479a-beb4-bb339cd293ee.pdf.

- ○ **Curation:** Independent booksellers began to focus on curating inventory in a way that allowed them to provide a more personal and specialized customer experience. Rather than simply recommending bestsellers, they developed personal relationships with customers by helping them discover up-and-coming authors and unexpected titles.

- ○ **Convening:** Independent booksellers also started to promote their stores as intellectual centers for convening customers with like-minded interests—offering lectures, book signings, game nights, children's story times, young adult reading groups, even birthday parties. "In fact, some bookstores now host over 500 events a year that bring people together," Raffaelli says.

This list will come as no surprise to booksellers and others in the book business. We've been doing these things for years. We may have called them *community involvement, selecting and promoting titles,* and *store events*, but they were fundamental to who we were and what we did.

The Vital Art of Curation

Curating, or selecting what books an independent store will carry, I should emphasize at the beginning, is an activity that values the diverse, varied, and heterogeneous. There are many different perspectives among indies on what buying, selecting, or curating means and how it should be done. In fact, whenever a group of booksellers is together to talk business, involved discussions of these topics will inevitably come up. One of the values of independent bookstores as a group is the wide range of people who select what books will be available to readers. There is a magic in having many minds involved in getting books from authors to readers, rather than having a few people who make determinations for everyone.

There are stores like City Lights in San Francisco, and many specialty stores, with a political or cultural point of view that is obvious in their title selection. Often these stores lean toward a progressive perspective. There have been new stores opened in the last few years with diverse owners from groups that have been historically under-represented in the book business. Their connections to the community are deeply rooted. Black-owned bookstores, both established and new, have brought new attention to books by and about Black people with the rise of the Black Lives Matter movement. (You can find a list of Black-owned independent bookstores on oprahdaily.com.) There are a growing number of bookstores focusing on LGBTQ+ books, as well as other kinds of bookstores with a wide range of diverse ownership and focus. (Find a list at diversebooks.org.)

There are also stores that combine commitments both to progressive ideas and to making a wide range of opinions available, regardless of how controversial. A. David Schwartz, when he owned the Harry W. Schwartz bookstores in Milwaukee, wrote, "Bookselling was and is for me a cultural and political expression, an expression of progressive change, of challenge to oppressive authority, of a search for a community of values which can act as an underpinning of a better world." He did not find any conflict between this view and a commitment to freedom of expression. Similarly, the store where I worked for over 40 years, Harvard Book Store in Cambridge, Massachusetts, crafted a mission statement in the 1980s stating that we "offer a carefully chosen and well-maintained selection that celebrates the perspective of diverse cultures. We honor literary traditions as we make available new voices and new ideas," and that we had a responsibility for "protecting freedom of expression."

Curation is necessary because no store can carry every book in print. Yet there are many bookstores that with great intentionality carry a wide range of books with differing perspectives, believing that to represent the spectrum of ideas is an important part of what a bookstore should do. Powell's Books in Portland, Oregon, Elliott Bay Book Company in Seattle, BookShop Santa Cruz in California, The Kings English in Salt Lake City, and Village Books in Bellingham, Washington, are only a few of the well-known stores that will usually stock any title, regardless of how controversial. Joyce Meskis and Tattered Cover belong to this tradition. Under her leadership, the store's mission was to carry as wide a range of books, including those with political viewpoints, as could fit on their shelves.

Joyce was in a league of her own on these matters, with a fierce commitment to free speech. Her dedication to what she believed bookselling should be was legendary. As booksellers know, there can be repercussions from across the political spectrum about the books a store does or does not stock, as we saw in the response to the *fatwa* issued against Salman Rushdie when his *Satanic Verses* was published. In the face of all attempts to limit what the store sold, Joyce was steadfast in her commitment to making available as wide a selection as possible. It made Tattered Cover one of the most famous and respected bookstores in the country.

I was a bookstore buyer for about thirty years, and to my mind selecting or curating the inventory that a store will stock, is one of the best jobs in the world as well as one of the major ways a bookstore is connected to the community. Great buyers buy *for* their customers. I was always envious of buyers I talked to who lived in places small enough that they knew many of their customers and what their interests were. Since I lived in a city and knew fewer customers personally, I came up with the idea of creating imaginary customers. I imagined a collection of composite customers, voracious readers all, and I selected books I knew they would like. One, of course, was a woman with tastes very much like mine. Another was a man a little younger than I am, very interested in science and math, philosophy, and history, but also a reader of literary fiction, sports books, and thrillers and espionage. In what seemed to me an extraordinary coincidence, when the long-time owner of the store put it up for sale, it turned out this imaginary customer was real, and he bought the store. A happy event all around.

When I say indie bookstores buy *for* our customers, I don't mean we buy only what we know our clientele will like. We also make available, and promote, books and authors we think people *should* know about. One of the things that always amazed and delighted me was that, whenever I got caught up in some new issue or topic and began buying more books in that field as I developed a clearer understanding of what was important, the new titles we stocked seemed to attract people who were interested in the subject. It's very hard for a buyer at an online national company to create that bond with readers, but for buyers at independent bookstores, it's a regular occurrence.

An important part of curation is staff recommendations. In most indie bookstores there will be short reviews written or printed on small cards that stick out from under books, written and signed by booksellers on the staff. In some stores there is a separate section dedicated to "Our Staff Recommends," and it's often the fastest selling section in the store. I'm sure that in indie stores a spot in the staff recommendation area is not for sale. Publishers can't influence the selection except by their enthusiasm for a book that convinces a bookseller to read it. The choices and recommendations are made solely by the bookseller. These recommendations are among the most powerful tools for promoting a book that I know of.

Convening—How Booksellers Bring Authors and Readers Together

What Raffaelli has called "convening"—bringing readers together and creating a sense of community—entails creating inviting spaces where ideas can be shared. Indie booksellers think carefully about the design of their stores, striving to create spaces that are welcoming and distinctive. Stores are as individual as the people who create them, often quirky, never corporate. It is striking to read customers' Yelp reviews of bookstores and notice how often people mention creaky floors, cozy nooks, bright and spacious layout, elegant design, or warm atmosphere. The best indie bookstores create a sense of place, from the sophistication of McNally Jackson stores in New York City, to the New England feel of An Unlikely Story Bookstore on the site of the historic Falk's Market in Plainville, Massachusetts, to the sense of Southern literary tradition that surrounds you at Square Books in Oxford, Mississippi.

The most common way of convening is the time-honored author event. Tattered Cover was a pioneer, one of the earliest stores to offer author appearances on a frequent and regular basis. I was in one of their stores recently, and dozens of beautiful photographs of great authors when they were much younger lined the walls of a staircase, a testament to how long the store has been featuring authors and to the amazing events they have hosted. A store gets such important authors by putting on great events that draw crowds, sell books, and make authors happy, and as with everything the Tattered Cover did, the events were extraordinary. Carefully planned, skillfully promoted, and meticulously executed, they were welcoming, warm, interesting, and almost invariably came off without a hitch.

In recent decades, as more indie bookstores looked for ways to connect to their communities and differentiate themselves from big box and online booksellers, bringing readers and authors together was an obvious approach. The author events that started in the 1970s became ubiquitous and numerous. Harvard Book Store, among other stores, offered over 500 events a year. Although authors often have a love/hate relationship with author tours and the sometimes onerous travel involved, they understand and appreciate the many ways that indie bookstores bring authors and readers together, including many authors

beyond those who write bestsellers. The result is often a deep bond between authors and the booksellers who support them. As Richard Russo
puts it in his introduction to *My Bookstore: Writers Celebrate Their
Favorite Places to Browse, Read and Shop,* "Many people love good
bookstores, but writers? We completely lose our heads over them . . .
because it's the independent bookseller who always gets the word out
(as they did for me). With their help . . . great young writers you don't
know about yet will take their place on shelves next to their heroes. . . .
Without them, well, I shudder to think."

Over time, new ideas for convening beyond author events have
blossomed. For example, Harvard Book Store hosted an inauguration-
watching party when Barack Obama became president. Frugal
Bookstore in Boston offers the NoName Book Club, a hybrid
online/real life community they describe as "dedicated to uplifting
voices by people of color . . . by highlighting two books each month written by authors of color. In addition to building community with folks
across the country we also send our monthly book picks to incarcerated
comrades through our Prison Program." Politics & Prose in Washington, D.C., offers in-store seminars led by local authors and academics.
Book Passage in Corta Madera, California, has a long history of offering
classes, including numerous presentations on writing. BookPeople in
Austin, Texas, created Literary Summer Camps, the first being Camp
Half-Blood, based on the Percy Jackson series by Rick Riordan, and
branching out to include the Ranger's Apprentice Corps Training
Camp, inspired by Australian author John Flanagan's medieval fantasy
series.

The list of innovative ways of connecting with readers is endless.
At stores across the country there are book club meetings, story hours,
book talks, symposia, debates, poetry slams, store events focused on
children's books, books on feminism, Black history and literature, cookbooks, LGBTQ+ issues, romance novels, mysteries, science fiction and
fantasy, books in translation, and more. Stores partner with local

cultural institutions like libraries and museums to expand events beyond the space in the store. Convening local book lovers has become a mainstay of independent bookselling, and something that no one else can do as well.

New technologies have also helped booksellers maintain connections with their customers, both local and remote, and many stores have regular email newsletters and a robust presence on social media. Booksellers connect readers and authors virtually as well. A number of bookstores produce and host radio shows, among them Thatcher Mountain Radio Hour from Square Books in Oxford, Mississippi, and the Chuckanut Radio Hour from Village Books in Bellingham, Washington.

Community: Booksellers in the Vanguard of the Localism Movement

In Rafaelli's research, *community* has a more specific meaning than that of building ties to a community as I've been discussing. He focuses particularly on booksellers' involvement in the Shop Local Movement. Localism has had a significant impact by educating communities about the importance of supporting local economies. Thanks to the circulation of data about the economic impact of shopping locally and the popularity of slogans like "put your money where your house is," more and more people are coming to understand that where they shop affects the health of their communities.

Booksellers have been founders and leaders of organizations that champion localism. Frank Kramer, the owner of Harvard Book Store, was instrumental in founding Shop Local First in Cambridge. David Bolduc, owner of the Boulder Bookstore, was a founding member of the Boulder Independent Business Alliance (one of the first of its kind in the country). He was at the forefront of the "shop local" movement and helped found the American Independent Business Alliance (AMIBA), which used Boulder as a test market for many programs. Betsy Burton, co-founder of The King's English in Salt Lake City, has been an activist in all things local. She co-founded Local First Utah and has served as its board chair since its inception. She has also travelled around the country offering workshops on how to start a local business alliance. BookPeople in Austin pioneered work with outside economic forecasting firms to measure the dollar impact of shopping locally and coined the slogan "Keep Austin Weird." Chuck Robinson of Village Books was one of the forces behind the Business Alliance for Local Living Economies (BALLE), one of the first national organizations to promote local economies.

Other bookstores that were early leaders in the localism movement include Anderson's Bookshop outside of Chicago; Changing Hands in Tempe, Arizona; Northshire Bookstore in Manchester Center, Vermont; Watermark Books and Cafe in Wichita, Kansas; and Quail Ridge Books in Raleigh, North Carolina. Today there are many more Local First leaders among booksellers across the country. This is not surprising, since booksellers are often involved in the leadership of their local communities. They have been mayors and have served on city councils, boards of selectmen, and school boards.

Booksellers as Community-Building Champions

Booksellers have also been active in protecting freedom of expression, and in 2024 they are working against the unprecedented number of state laws banning books and infringing on the Constitutional rights of readers. This involvement has a long history. In 1953, because of attacks on books led by Senator Joseph McCarthy, the American Library Association and the Association of American Publishers first unveiled the Freedom to Read Statement, which begins, "The freedom to read is essential to our democracy. It is continuously under attack." On its 70th anniversary in 2023, booksellers reaffirmed that statement.

Promoting literacy is another way in which booksellers have been involved in the larger community. In 1998, Roxanne Coady of RJ Julia Booksellers in Madison, Connecticut, founded Read To Grow, Inc., an organization that promotes development of early literacy and language skills, working to give all Connecticut children the tools for success in reading. Powell's Books has run an annual program called "It's for the Kids" which donates money to Portland, Oregon, schools. Booksellers have supported the national non-profit Reading Is Fundamental. These are only a sample of the many local efforts by bookstores to support and advance literacy.

Booksellers have played significant roles in political movements beyond selling books. One of the best examples among many is Marcus Books in Oakland, California, the oldest institution specializing in African American literature and history, which has long been a center for the Black community to celebrate and learn about its culture. Notable figures such as Malcolm X, Toni Morrison, Nikki Giovanni, Octavia Butler, and Maya Angelou have hosted readings there. And beyond being a renowned bookstore, Marcus Books played an integral role during the civil rights movement as a safe meeting space for activists to gather before and after protests.

Finally, I'd like to touch on the community of booksellers, which is indirectly connected to the role bookstores play in the larger community. Over the years, I've learned that booksellers are different from many other businesspeople in that we see fellow booksellers more as colleagues than competitors. There is a natural camaraderie among booksellers. Years ago, when there were twenty-three bookstores within six blocks of Harvard Square, buyers from the stores got together regularly. At least once a month we'd meet for drinks at a local restaurant and talk about business. We got to be friends. We were competitors, but we didn't think of each other in that way. We helped each other out, and we talked freely about our stores. Many of us participated in the educational programming offered by the regional and national trade associations, where people would share their trade secrets.

I remember talking to people outside the industry—people from corporate America, or people new to bookselling from other industries—and they were astounded. "So, you mean you just get up and tell everybody how to do what you do?" they would ask. And when I said, "Well . . . yes!" they didn't understand it. They thought it was crazy.

But we cared that there were many independent bookstores, and that communities were served by local bookstores that were connected with their lives. This sense of fellowship is probably not unique to the book business, but it's certainly unusual. And no one was more important in fostering the community of booksellers than Joyce Meskis. In fact, I first met her when we taught together at the Booksellers Schools that were offered in those days by the American Booksellers Association. Although she was already a legend in the industry, she treated all of us as peers, and was so warm and down-to-earth that she put everyone at ease. Her work in the Mountains and Plains regional booksellers association led to her involvement in ABA, where she became president.

Building on the great traditions I've described, in recent years independent bookstores have been expanding the communities they reach, beyond the readers who live close to them. This was a paradoxical benefit of the Covid-19 pandemic, which brought new attention to local businesses. Most bookstores already had websites and were selling books online, but with a few exceptions it was a small part of the indie book business. In March of 2020, when many bookstores were mandated to close their doors to in-person shoppers, they were inundated with questions from readers who wanted to buy from them online. For many stores, their online sales became the biggest part of their business and remained important even after they reopened to in-store customers.

During the pandemic, numerous indie bookstores became masters of virtual author events, and as the pandemic has receded, many stores, including Harvard Book Store, have continued to host both in-person and virtual events. As an added benefit, video records of virtual events are often available on a store's website long after the event. As I write this, Mahogany Books, a Black-owned store in Washington, D.C., offers Front Row, a virtual author series with authors including Misty Copeland, the Reverend Al Sharpton, Van Jones, and Kwame Alexander. All these events are still available for viewing.

In addition, bookstore podcasts have proliferated, notably those from Books & Books in Florida, Greenlight Bookstore in Brooklyn, Boswell Book Company in Milwaukee, and RJ Julia in Madison, Connecticut, among others.

Bookstore tourism is now "a thing," even having an entry in Wikipedia, and indie bookstores cooperate in creating tours that visit bookstores in many cities and regions. More broadly, full-blown literary tours of sites important in cultural history led by booksellers include author events, literary walking tours, museum and gallery tours led by expert local guides, and excellent food and drink. Among others, Rainy Day Books in Fairway, Kansas, has led groups to England and Italy, Politics & Prose has offered trips to Paris and Istanbul, and BookPeople of Moscow, Idaho, has taken a group to Tuscany.

Booksellers have always participated in local book festivals, but there are now festivals that have national or regional audiences, many of them founded and spearheaded by booksellers and with independent bookstores handling book sales. One of the most famous is the Miami Book Fair International, begun in 1984 by Miami-Dade College and local booksellers, and now presenting hundreds of authors over several days. The National Book Festival in Washington, D.C., organized and sponsored by the Library of Congress, was founded by former librarian Laura Bush and Librarian of Congress James H. Billington in 2001 and has Politics & Prose as its the official bookstore. The relatively young

Boston Book Festival, founded as an independent nonprofit in 2009, is a one-day festival with hundreds of authors in multiple venues. The largest festival, the Los Angeles Times Festival of Books, began in 1996 with a goal of bringing together "the people who create books with the people who love to read them." The festival has evolved to include live bands, poetry readings, film screenings and artists creating their work on-site. Again, local bookstores handle book sales.

AS I'VE SHOWN IN THESE PAGES, the vital role of bookstores in our culture and our communities is multifaceted and grows more so every day. Perhaps no one appreciates this or expresses it more eloquently than the writers whose books we sell.

In describing his favorite bookstore, Rick Atkinson writes that it "remains nothing less than the bricks-and-mortar incarnation of traits we cherish in Western civilization: learning, tolerance, diversity, civility, discourse, inquiry, lyricism." And writing about her own favorite bookstore, Isabel Allende adds, "This shop is the cultural soul of a large community."

Pico Iyer in talking about independent bookstores says, "A bookshop isn't just about business, it's about shared passion. It's a conversation, a spirited exchange." He continues, "It's not so much what passes between hands at the cash register that matters so much, as what passes between minds."

Emily St. John Mandel, in her afterword to *My Bookstore*, points out the individuality of independent bookstores, the "personalities and eccentricities of their owners, managers, and staff; if at least one of the reasons to read is to expand the mind, a point is being missed here; independent bookstores are personal . . . things happen in bookstores that don't happen in other places where we buy books."

There is among booksellers a sense that the work we do is important to our communities, and we take pride in that work. We believe there is a cultural and social responsibility inherent in what we do. Bookstore staff, who could often make more money working somewhere else, have an unusual commitment to their work, and to the importance of books.

Mandel's "things that happen" occur because bookstores at their best are, as Richard Russo says, "places of genuine wonder." They are places of discovery because someone has selected the books with passion; they are anchors in a fragile democracy because someone has stood up to attempts to limit what we can read; they are oases of inclusion because a multitude of voices can be found there. Bookstores serve as community centers, town squares, and safe havens. I remember on September 11, 2001, soon after we opened at 9:00 a.m., our store started to fill up. People were looking for information, and we quickly put together a display of books that seemed relevant to the situation. But more than information, they simply wanted to be with other people with whom they sensed a connection, and the bookstore felt like the place to go. Bookstores are community destinations and institutions, part of the fabric of life. As George Whitman, who opened the current iteration of Shakespeare & Company in Paris in 1951, said, "the business of books is the business of life."

You'll remember that earlier I quoted David Schwartz: "Bookselling was and is for me a cultural and political expression, an expression of progressive change, of challenge to oppressive authority, of a search for a community of values which can act as an underpinning of a better world." He finishes by saying, "The true profit in bookselling is the social profit; the bottom line, the measure of the impact of the bookshop on the community." I wish I'd said that.

PART TWO

The Business of Books

7.
The Mentorship of
an Aspiring Publisher

Jack Jensen

Jack Jensen joined Chronicle Books in 1977 as Western States sales representative when the company had six employees and published 12 titles per year. He was later promoted to sales and marketing director and in 1991 was named president and publisher of Chronicle. Jensen was the chief architect in transforming Chronicle from a small regional press to one of the country's largest independent publishers, which today publishes more than three hundred titles annually in categories including children's books, cookbooks, art, photography, lifestyle, pop culture, humor, wellness, stationery, gift, and games. In May 2023, Jensen retired from his position as president of Chronicle's parent company the McEvoy Group. He assumed the chairmanship of of the McEvoy Group advisory board and continues to serve on the board of Chronicle's U.K.-based joint venture with Abrams, Abrams & Chronicle Books.

T HE RETAIL EXPERIENCE Joyce Meskis created at the Tattered Cover was suffused with numerous attributes, and they all emanated from one core principle: serving the customer well. Joyce and her Tattered Cover colleagues burnished this principle over her entire career, and it evolved in ways that even she could not have imagined. I was lucky enough to know Joyce for over 40 years and to learn from her as a publishing industry colleague—first as a book salesman, then as a publisher. I am honored to share some of the lessons I learned from Joyce over those 40 wonderful years.

The special qualities of the Tattered Cover started with the people Joyce hired. She had very solid instincts when it came to judging character and talent. Loving books and the world of books was an essential quality in potential employees, but it was by no means sufficient. They also had to be comfortable in their own skin and have the ability to listen carefully to others, submerging their own tastes and instincts in favor of discovering what the customer was after.

A Tattered Cover team member had to accept the importance of mastering every aspect of the bookselling endeavor, recognizing that the true test of success was a satisfied customer. Joyce understood that many potential customers were intimidated when entering a bookstore, concerned that they and their interests might not be perceived as "up to snuff." As a consequence, Joyce insisted that staff members never pass judgment on a customer's request.

In short, the ideal bookseller had to be attentive, thoughtful, and above all passionately driven by a desire to serve the customer.

New team members at Tattered Cover started work with a rigorous training course. When they were finally ready to work the floor, they spent their first day shadowing Joyce's own interactions with customers so they could witness first-hand the type of service she wanted her customers to receive. She made this happen when she managed a staff of five people, and mostly made it happen even after the head count ballooned to four hundred. Not every new hire proved to be a success, but the customer-driven culture at Tattered Cover was so profound that those who failed to embody it moved on in short order.

The insistence on customer-centricity extended well beyond the exemplary customer service provided by the floor staff, and the backstage crew was where the Tattered Cover's distinct identity really shined. For example, when it came to acquiring inventory, Joyce left the buying decisions to her staff, but she made it clear that the titles selected should reflect the widest breadth of interest possible.

The world is filled with endless stories, ideas, and pursuits, and the goal of the Tattered Cover was to represent as many of them as possible. Over the years, the title count grew as prodigiously as the square footage of the store in Denver's Cherry Creek neighborhood. Non-book sidelines were scarce and were mostly related to the world of reading and writing. There was also an exceptionally diverse offering of periodicals from all over the world. In short, the Tattered Cover was designed to be a paradise for lovers of reading, where practically every taste could be satisfied.

The physical design of the store reinforced the same message. From day one, the Tattered Cover's environment offered an oasis of comfort. The dark shelving helped to frame the books, creating an eye-pleasing air of excitement and curiosity. The floor plan included numerous nooks and crannies, providing the customer with a sense of adventure and discovery, and the furnishings exuded extraordinary style and comfort, begging the customer to pull a book from a shelf and take a seat.

As a result, customers would literally spend hours in the store, and while they did not always leave with an armful of books, they did come back, often with friends or family to share the experience. There was never a reprimand when students pulled books from the shelves and sat on the floor copying text for their homework. Children loved the kids' rooms, with their colorful furnishings and books strewn about as they might appear in their own homes. It's no wonder that any number of wonderful romances and more than a few marriages found their genesis at the Tattered Cover.

As I came to discover, Joyce's home was always a bastion of warmth and comfort, but the furnishings were less grand than those in her store. When I asked her once how she could afford to lavish such extravagance on her business, she quickly replied, "The customers need to feel wanted." Joyce dedicated herself to making sure they did. Whenever she managed to take some time off, she could often be found scouting for just the right pieces to enhance the look of the store even further, and her taste was impeccable.

Joyce did nothing halfway. During the years when the Tattered Cover was growing, food and drink were finding their way into many bookstores, and there had always been a modest coffee bar at the store. But Joyce wasn't satisfied with just another eatery. She decided that the Tattered Cover should offer a "proper" dining experience, and so she devoted the entire fourth floor of the store to a fine dining establishment that served excellent meals at both lunch and dinner. The Fourth Story Restaurant & Bar graced many top-ten Denver restaurant lists for years, and the store benefitted from the multitude of customers that dined there.

Reflecting on the customer experience that Joyce and her multitude of talented colleagues created, it's stunningly obvious that the analog jewel that was the Cherry Creek Tattered Cover provided service that was light years ahead of the digital shopping mall that now dominates our retail landscape and endlessly boasts that it is customer-centric.

I started my career in the book business during my college years, when I worked as a bookseller with B. Dalton. In 1977, I was offered a job with San Francisco-based Chronicle Books. At the time, the staff totaled five people, and while we all did a bit of everything, my job title was Western States Sales Representative—which meant that work included calling on the Tattered Cover. The store was still located at its initial Second Avenue location, and the staff was approximately 10 people. Joyce was always clearly present, but my main interactions were with the buyers.

I was new to publishing but not to bookselling, and I was immediately impressed with the friendly but professional approach the staff at the Tattered Cover brought to their work. After my first few sales calls, I decided I had to become better acquainted with the quietly ambitious proprietor of this distinctive store. So the next time I called to schedule a sales appointment, I asked if I could be switched over to Joyce. When I invited her to go to lunch on my upcoming visit, she replied, "My days are far too busy to go out to lunch. But I'd be happy to have you come to my home for dinner."

I was caught off guard by the invitation. The Chronicle Books of those days was a small player in the publishing world. In retrospect, it was precisely our small size and West Coast location that appealed to Joyce. We enjoyed one another's company, and thus began a long string of dinners at her home in Littleton, Colorado, along with her daughters Katherine and Julie. After dinner we would be immersed in conversation about the profoundly exciting work of making and selling books. I learned that Joyce had originally been a librarian, and that she had experienced a disheartening loss when her first bookstore start-up failed prematurely due to its location in a newly constructed but short-lived suburban development.

We shared our experiences stewarding rapidly-growing businesses. It was then I learned about Joyce's customer-first mantra, as well as her belief that building a dedicated and diverse group of booksellers was essential to the success of an independent bookstore. Diversity, equity, and inclusion were core values that Joyce embraced and embodied long before they became fashionable, much less mandatory. These evenings together were both fun and enlightening, and the food and beverages were terrific as well.

As the early years of our relationship progressed, I realized that in addition to building an enduring friendship I was learning important aspects of what it took to be a success in the book business. Joyce was emerging as the recognized leader of the independent bookselling community, and she was passionately committed to seeing that the independent publishing community—those who were not part of the New York conglomerates—were well represented to the book-buying public.

It became clear to me that we at Chronicle Books could better differentiate our future publishing and go-to-market strategies if we focused more on what our customers—both retailers as well as the ultimate consumers, readers—were looking for, rather than relying solely on the judgment of our editors and marketing people. Market-driven publishing could indeed be distinctive and successful publishing if it was informed by a deep understanding of the consumer. Joyce and the team she created offered a picture-perfect model for this way of thinking.

By the late 1980s, Chronicle Books was growing as fast as the Tattered Cover, and I moved on from the role of sales representative to that of publisher. Nonetheless, it was clear to me that I wanted to continue to nurture my relationship with Joyce and to stay aligned with her always inspiring business. So even while serving as publisher, I continued to be the Chronicle Books sales representative for Tattered Cover for the following 30 years.

It was a blast to watch the meteoric growth in Cherry Creek, but it was even more wonderful to witness the Tattered Cover's expansion into the burgeoning neighborhood of Lower Downtown Denver (LoDo). In addition to creating a second one-of-a-kind destination bookstore, Joyce joined forces with then-brew pub owner John Hickenlooper to undertake urban development opportunities. Mercantile Square became the home of a new 35,000-square-foot Tattered Cover as well as other commercial storefronts and an array of market-rate and subsidized housing.

Joyce and her new spouse Jed Rulon-Miller were living nearby in a splendid loft above the Wynkoop Brew Pub, where a whole new round of evenings began with Joyce, Jed, and often Jed's school days chum John Hickenlooper. If possible, the food got even better, and the libations now included offerings from Wines off Wynkoop, Jed's new enterprise, in which I became a small but proud investor, as well as a freshly brewed keg of craft beer from the brew pub downstairs. Our dinner conversations were as animated as ever, mostly centered around the ever-growing businesses we were stewarding. Our worldviews were similar, so we invariably got down to stipulating the good guys and bad guys in culture and politics.

On the business side there was one area where Joyce and I did not quite see eye to eye. I have always believed that books are underserved in the retail landscape, and thus felt it was imperative for publishers to expand the retail customer base for their list of titles. Books are highly valued in our culture, but, for any number of reasons, many consumers rarely, if ever, enter a bookstore. Chronicle Books began building a reputation for placing books throughout the retail landscape, making use of "special markets" that included everything from hardware stores to car washes. My rationale was that it was our job to get books in the hands of all consumers, including those who were new to books, and so to grow the overall number of book consumers.

Joyce had a different perspective. She thought it was all well and good that we had stacks of our food titles at cookware stores, but she worried about treating books as products, which would, in the long run, devalue both books and bookstores. When that happened, exactly who did we expect to represent our newest collection of poetry, or an arcane but useful reference title?

She was right—books were indeed becoming more and more "commoditized," and independent booksellers had to contend with both large chain bookstores and an ever-growing Amazon presence. Making matters worse, the latest bestsellers—the bread and butter of independent bookstores—were seemingly available everywhere, from drugstores to big box retailers, and, more often than not, at heavily dis-counted prices. I empathized with the struggles of the indie booksellers, but I stood by my premise that the more retailers carrying books, the better. For me, now as then, more retailers selling books eventually means more readers buying books.

On this point, Joyce and I agreed to disagree. Years later, when I made a presentation at the Denver Publishing Institute about market diversification as a central pillar of Chronicle Books's publishing strat-egy, Joyce took me aside later in the day and confided that she finally understood my perspective and dearly hoped we were right. Coming from Joyce, I took that as a victory.

Our friendship went well beyond our shared profession. We both knew one another's families, and over the years Joyce visited me in San Francisco where I got to share my home, friends, and family with her.

The book *The Tattered Cover Bookstore: A Storied History* by Mark A. Barnhouse commences with this 1984 quote from Joyce:

> I got into this business because I love books. I mean I *really* love books. That, to me, is what running a bookstore is about. Publishing and books are incredibly important to humanity. I really believe that. I think that if we don't fill our role of putting books in the hands of people who want to read them, it's al-most sinful.

For Joyce, the book business was a vocation rather than a career, and her contributions to the industry she so revered were multitudi-nous. She served as president of the American Booksellers Association at the height of the challenges independent booksellers were facing due to what were deemed unfair competitive practices by large publishers in favor of national chain stores. In this endeavor, she was the perfect spokesperson for fairness and equity on both sides.

When the Publishing Institute at the University of Denver needed new stewardship, she stepped forward to take the mantle, and given her beloved stature in the book publishing industry she was able to draw a vast array of talented publishing professionals to the Institute for its highly respected six-week graduate course.

Her customer-centric mantra was put to the test when the federal Drug Enforcement Agency demanded she turn over a customer's purchasing history because they suspected the person of drug dealing. She refused to comply, telling the agents that their request could not be met because the information they were demanding was private. As always, Joyce was putting her customer first. As the story unfolded, her polite but firm refusal to comply turned into a significant First Amendment battle in which she and readers nationwide ultimately prevailed.

These are just a few of the most commonly known contributions Joyce made to the business she so loved. But her most profound contribution was witnessed day in and day out by the vast array of people with whom she interacted. She took a sincere interest in everyone with whom she communicated. Humble and gracefully understated was how Joyce rolled. Always listening, always curious, and always empathetic.

Time with Joyce was always time well spent. She was indeed a cherished friend and an inspiring mentor in my publishing career as well as my life.

8.
Four Decades of Evolution in the Book Business

Chuck Robinson

Chuck Robinson was born and raised in a small Illinois farming com-munity. He earned his bachelor of arts degree from Sioux Falls College (now the University of Sioux Falls) and a master's degree from the University of Missouri . In 1980, after teaching and consulting in ed-ucation for ten years, Chuck, with his wife Dee, founded Village Books in Bellingham, Washington's historic Fairhaven District. Two years later they opened Paper Dreams, a card and gift store. In November of 2015, a second Village Books and Paper Dreams store was opened in Lynden, Washington. In January of 2017, the entire business was sold to three employees.

In addition to serving on the board of the American Booksellers Association for nine years and as its president for two years, Chuck has been a member of more than fifteen local and national nonprofit boards, including the Whatcom Community Foundation, Bellingham City Club, The Book Industry Charitable Foundation, and Sustainable Connections. He also served as a trustee of Whatcom Community Col-lege for ten years. He is the author of the book It Takes a Village Books:

35 Years of Building Community, One Book at a Time. *Chuck was named Man of the Year by the Bellingham Whatcom Chamber of Commerce, and the Bellingham Rotary Club presented him with the Paul Harris Award.*

I FIRST MET JOYCE MESKIS at an American Booksellers Association (ABA) convention in Washington, D.C., in the early 1980s, but I didn't really get to know her until we joined the board of ABA together in May 1987. During our years working together, Joyce became a good friend and my most trusted mentor. Much of the success that we experienced at Village Books over the next three decades was certainly influenced by her. Whenever I think about the many changes in the book business between 1980, when my wife Dee and I launched our store, and when we retired in 2017, I think of Joyce and how her leadership and mentorship helped so many booksellers adapt to those changes. Because of her, many of us survived and even thrived.

In memory of Joyce, I want to describe how, from my perspective, the landscape of publishing and bookselling has evolved since 1980. Individually some of the changes may seem insignificant, but the combination has left many segments of the industry far different than they were on that June day in 1980 when we opened our store. Many of the changes have been positive, though some have made operating an independent bookstore, never an easy task, more difficult. Some of the changes were inevitable, some might have been better avoided. And some things have never changed. As the French say, *Plus ça change, plus c'est la même chose* ("The more things change, the more they stay the same").

Publishing: Increased Consolidation,
Heightened Competition

From the perspective of 1980, the publishing side of the business today would be nearly unrecognizable. A business that had been run largely by editors has undergone a rapid transition to leadership by account-ants and business executives, often hired from outside the book busi-ness. While the change has brought business efficiencies, it has also largely shifted the focus of publishing to short-term returns and deci-sions based on expediency rather than quality publishing.

One of the areas of short-term focus has been on the books them-selves. The number of books published has exploded, with current esti-mates of the average number of titles published annually, including self-published as well as traditionally published books, hovering around three million. Authors often complain that the moment their books come out of the bindery and (sometimes) get an initial launch, the publisher is on to the next book in line. A number of bestselling au-thors have resorted to hiring their own publicists and marketing ex-perts to fill perceived gaps in the services publishers provide.

Partly in response to these gaps, partly driven by new technologi-cal capabilities, self-publishing has mushroomed over the last ten years. A publishing model once limited mostly to local and regional in-terest titles now encompasses every category of books. According to Bowker, the company that issues the International Standard Book Number (ISBN) for each new book published, there were 2.3 million ISBNs issued for self-published books in 2021.

The 1980s were also the advent of rapid publisher consolidation, with well-known publishing names becoming imprints within larger companies. The merger that created Penguin Random House (PRH), the largest publisher in America, reduced what had been known as the Big Six U.S. publishers to the Big Five. Had an attempted merger of Si-mon & Schuster and PRH not been halted by the Justice Department in

2022, the number would have dwindled to four. The concentration of publishing in fewer companies is not just a U.S. phenomenon; giant PRH has its hand in publishing on all of the five most populated continents.

In a related trend, the 1980s saw the death knell of an era in which "over the transom" or unsolicited manuscripts had a realistic chance of being published by a traditional house. Its demise had begun in the late sixties, but by 1980 getting a general-interest book published without the help of an agent had become virtually impossible. What's more, finding an agent was becoming increasingly difficult. I recall a friend of mine, an author of numerous books, who had taken a break to sail the world. When he returned, he was frustrated to find he couldn't attract an agent to represent his future books. And as agents became more selective, they also became more powerful. Agents took on much of the role that in-house editors had formerly served, helping to shape books and performing early edits before submission to publishing houses.

Over these decades, author advances have also escalated. Publisher Peter Osnos, writing in an 2011 article in *The Atlantic*, recalled being authorized by the powers that be at Random House to go as high as $50,000 for a book by Geraldine Ferraro, the 1984 Democratic candidate for vice president. That book ultimately sold at auction for $1 million—a sizeable sum at the time. In fact, when Tip O'Neill's book *Man of the House* was sold in 1985 for a million, the transaction earned it a *New York Times* front-page story. Today, no one would blink at a $1 million advance for a high-profile book. Osnos notes that Bill and Hillary Clinton reportedly received a combined $20 million for the books they wrote following Bill's terms as president.

New Book Formats and New Ways of Delivering Content

Moving downstream, the changes in bookselling have been as dramatic as those in publishing. Four decades ago, the fastest way for a bookstore to get books was through wholesale distributors, both regional and national. However, those outlets had limited titles available, and obtaining books directly from publishers took much more time than it does today, especially for stores like Village Books, located on the West Coast. As so-called just-in-time inventory management gained popularity, nearly every major publisher greatly reduced its shipping times, allowing more books to be ordered directly. Some publishers now air freight books during the busy holiday season, getting books to bookstores in as little as two days. This more efficient delivery system allows stores to better utilize their inventory dollars by stocking just enough copies of a book to satisfy projected sales over a shorter period of time.

In 1980, the paperback sections of bookstores, both in fiction and nonfiction, were dominated by mass market format books—small books, typically six and three quarters by four and a quarter inches in size, a format common since the 1930s. Though larger format paperbacks, called "trade paperbacks," had been around since the 1960s, they were not very prevalent. That began to change in 1984, when Random House published *Bright Lights, Big City* by Jay McInerney as an original large format paperback. It sold extremely well and helped make trade or "quality paperbacks" popular. Today, trade paperbacks make up the bulk of the books in the fiction and nonfiction sections of most stores.

The audio book is another format that has changed dramatically in the past four decades. In 1980, audio books were delivered primarily on cassette tapes. During that decade, they began moving onto compact discs (CDs), which were popular among commuters in urban markets and among road trippers and folks who could listen on Walkmans while exercising or doing repetitive work, such as mending fishing nets, in rural markets like the one we served in Washington state. Now most audio books are sold as digital downloads, and their numbers are sky-rocketing, The Audio Publishers Association reported ten straight years of double-digit increases in the sales of audio books between 2011 and 2021, with the total number of books published in audio increasing in those same years from 7,200 to 74,000.

At first, the audiobook boom left bookstores largely out in the cold. With the digital company Audible holding a huge share of the market, consumers of audio books had few choices of where to buy their books, and independent bookstores had little opportunity to sell digital audio books. That changed in 2013 when Libro.fm launched a partnership program for independent bookstores. Those partnerships have grown from 150 store partnerships in 2016 to more than 1,500 stores in 2024.

Digital distribution has also revolutionized the market for tradi-tional non-audio books. Electronic books were first created as long ago as the 1930s, but 1998 is considered a major turning point in their pop-ularization. In that year, ISBNs began to be issued for ebooks, the first e-readers appeared, libraries began lending ebooks, and Google was founded. When ebooks began claiming a significant share of the read-ing market, some predicted the eventual disappearance of printed books. But the growth curve for ebooks leveled off, and today, twenty-five years later, print books, according to the American Association of Publishers, still account for about 75 percent of books sales while the ebook share is slightly above ten percent. About a third of readers say they read in both print and ebook formats, and less than ten percent of readers claim that they read ebooks exclusively.

Again, it took a while for booksellers to get in on the digital action. Early on, it was virtually impossible for independent bookstores to sell ebooks, and it was more than ten years until Google made ebooks avail-able through indy stores. Later Kobo introduced a digital reader and ebooks that indies could sell. Today there are several sources of ebooks available through independent bookstores.

Changes Inside the Bookstore

The average size of bookstores has vacillated over the years. We opened our store in 1980 in 1,500 square feet, which was likely close to the average size of bookstores at the time, including the two main chain stores, Waldenbooks and B. Dalton. The Tattered Cover in Denver started out close in size to the original Village Books, then grew into one of the first book megastores when it opened its Cherry Creek location in 1986. Though the chain megastores are the most familiar, there were also very large independent stores in other cities, including Dayton, Atlanta, and the original Borders store in Ann Arbor, an indy store created in 1971 by brothers Tom and Louis Borders. As for Village Books, over the years, it grew to be more than 10,000 square feet. Today many independent bookstores are around 3,000 to 4,000 square feet, and larger stores still exist. Though the Tattered Cover has reduced its square footage, it has multiple stores.

Sidelines, as non-book products in the bookselling business are called, have become a much more prominent part of most bookstores over the years. In 1980, it was uncommon for a bookstore to have more than 10 percent of its sales in sidelines. Today, nearly every bookstore has a larger percentage than that, and many derive more than 30 percent of their inventory and sales from sidelines. The increase has been driven by the need for products with higher profit margins than books as well as the desire to attract a wider range of customers. The types of products have also changed greatly, moving from mostly book-related items—bookmarks, reading lights, book covers, greeting cards, and such—to a wide variety of merchandise, including socks, T-shirts, cooking items, jewelry, candy, and much more.

There have long been interesting bookstore hybrids such as the long-gone Freddy's Feed and Read in Missoula, Montana, a combination bookstore, organic market, and vegetarian restaurant. However, the number of such hybrids has increased in recent years. The most common combination has been the bookstore café. In 1985, when Village Books partnered with the Colophon Café, there weren't many such amalgamations around the country. Today bookstore cafés are ubiquitous. Incorporating bars into bookstores, such as First Draft Book Bar in Phoenix, Rough Draft Bar & Books in Kingston, New York, and Book Club Bar in New York City, to name just a few, has been a growing phenomenon.

Before the mid-1980s, very few independent bookstores used computers, and dedicated bookstore computer systems were very limited; two systems shared most of the nascent market. The adoption of computer inventory management and point-of-sale systems grew rapidly in the following ten years, until it became uncommon for bookstores to operate without them. There was resistance among some booksellers, who felt that the technology was at odds with the literary nature of the business. However, even the most hard-core Luddites became converts as inventory management and customer service became more efficient.

Meanwhile, the 1980s saw the demise of book sections in department stores and office supply stores. When we opened our store, the Fredrick and Nelson department store in Seattle had a very large book section. Likewise, J.K. Gill, a Western states chain of office supply stores, had a significant presence in the book business. Even in our smaller town of Bellingham, the local stationery store dedicated a large section of one floor to books. This was a common pattern from coast to coast. Competition from book retailers likely contributed to the demise of those book departments. Interestingly, a number of Northwest booksellers who'd gotten started in those other businesses continued in the book industry, working for wholesalers, other book retailers, or opening bookstores of their own.

Giant Players Enter the Fray,
and the Independents Bounce Back

Then there's the story of the big bookstore chains. By 1985, Waldenbooks and B. Dalton Bookseller had become major players in the retail book business, with hundreds of mall-based stores dotting the country. Waldenbooks, which K-Mart had purchased in 1984, was then the largest book chain. Eight years later K-Mart purchased the Borders stores. After struggling to operate the book division, K-Mart spun off the bookstores. What became the Borders Group continued to operate the stores until 2011, when, after filing for bankruptcy, it closed its remaining stores.

B. Dalton Bookseller had been founded in 1966 by Bruce Dayton, a member of the family that owned Dayton's department stores. By 1986, the chain had 798 locations, mostly in malls. That year, Dayton Hudson sold the stores to Barnes & Noble, which by 2013 closed all of the B. Dalton locations. While competition no doubt played a part in the decline of the stores, the erosion of mall business also was a significant factor.

The year 1995 brought the biggest change to book retailing in more than a century. That was when Amazon embarked on its online retailing venture. Books were the product chosen to launch the business, but as we all later discovered, the long-term vision was to be an online retailer of a multitude of products and services. Because books were not perishable, were selected by title and not color or size, and shipped easily, they were an ideal choice for entrepreneur Jeff Bezos's first experiment in digital marketing. As books are one of very few products that have indelible printed prices, they were also an ideal item for discounting.

It wasn't long before other Amazon products eclipsed books in both sales and profits—in fact, it's unclear whether book sales have ever been profitable for Amazon. Yet the company is still viewed as a bookseller. Very narrow profit margins in books have made it difficult for booksellers to compete with the discounts being offered by the online behemoth. As Amazon grew, many independent stores were either forced or chose to shut down their businesses.

I love to tell folks that Village Books was selling books online before Amazon. It's true. In the early 1990s, the store sold books for social work classes at the local university using a flat database online. The process was nothing like the one later launched by the now humongous Seattle company, and it was some time before Village Books and other independent booksellers began selling a wide variety of books online. One major turning point for indies came at the turn of the century, when the ABA debuted its own online bookselling platform. (The platform was totally revamped and renamed IndieCommerce in 2009.)

While this platform democratized the selling of books online, most indies still sold a very small percentage of their books that way. However, the Covid-19 pandemic of 2020-21 brought about a huge surge in online book sales for independent stores. According to the ABA, online sales of independent bookstores have increased 580 percent since 2020, contributing more than $200 million in revenue for those stores. In 2022, ABA poured more than $2 million into upgrading the online selling system. In addition, ABA has taken an ownership position in bookshop.org, which allows any bookstore to sell books online and receive 30 percent of the sale, at no cost to the bookseller. Small stores without their own online sales system as well as larger stores using the system as an additional sales nexus have earned more than $26 million from the system since its beginning in 2020.

Beginning with the advent of Amazon and continuing through the 2008 recession, the number of independent bookstores dwindled from an estimated total of more than 3,500 to around half that. However, in recent years, hundreds of new stores have opened, and a large number of independent bookstores have opened second and third locations. In explaining the reasons for the independent bookstore resurgence, a Harvard Business School study by Ryan Raffaelli concluded that it was driven by three benefits that bookstores provide:

o   Bookstores build communities;
o   Bookstores emphasize the careful curation of books;
o   Bookstores become centers of convening in communities

These are three kinds of activities, built around the intellectual, social, and aesthetic values of books themselves, that only booksellers can offer.

Some of the new independent bookstore venues are freestanding, while some are within other businesses or organization. Airport stores, which in the past were largely chain operations, are now often either owned by independents or in partnership with independent stores. Pop-up locations, including seasonal stores, have also become popular, and several stores have added bookmobiles.

Village Books illustrates some of these alternative bookselling ventures. From 2000 until 2010, the store operated a bookmobile that visited small cities around our county and was present at a number of special events. After several mechanical issues and lack of serious revenue returns, it spent its final years as a billboard in a prominent spot along a major thoroughfare. In the fall of 2011 through January, 2012, the store managed a pop-up holiday store in a local mall. In November, 2015 a second location was opened in Lynden, a small city twenty miles north of our Fairhaven stores. Similar ventures continue across the country.

Village Books also illustrates Raffaeli's third bookstore benefit, the power to convene gatherings of people with shared interests. When our store opened in 1980, author visits to bookstores were not very common, especially in smaller cities, and most visits were simply signings. The next few years saw an explosion in author events as readings, talks, and interviews were added to the menu for bringing authors in contact with readers. Village Books helped fuel this trend. Three weeks after opening our store, we hosted the first author for a signing and a decision was made to make author events a key part of our marketing and interaction in the community. For a few years, we hosted four authors per quarter at the store. Over time, the number increased steadily, so when we exited the stores in 2017 there were more than three hundred author events occurring each year, often more than one a day and occasionally as many as four.

Village Books was not unique in this growth. The Tattered Cover, for example, far eclipsed the number of events we were doing. Multiple events each day became a common occurrence there and at other larger bookstores.

Technology Transforms Bookselling

Technology played a key role in some of the changes bookselling experienced.

In 1999, Jason Epstein, the renowned editorial director at Random House (1976-1995) and co-founder of *The New York Review of Books*, gave a far-sighted speech at the New York Public Library. In it, he envisioned a machine that would be available in bookstores, libraries, and even coffee shops that would print books on demand.

At the time, Epstein didn't realize that a prototype for such a machine already existed. Four years later, he and Dane Neller founded On Demand Books (ODB) and partnered with the inventor of that machine to produce the Espresso Book Machine. The first of those machines were installed in 2006 in the World Bank InfoShop in Washington, D.C., and the Library of Alexandria, Egypt. These were followed two years later by an Espresso Book Machine in Northshire Bookstore in Manchester Center, Vermont, the first independent bookstore to install one. Village Books was the third, quickly followed by a number of other independent stores.

In the time that Village Books operated its Espresso Book Machine, hundreds of books were printed using files available from Google and publishers; dozens of authors self-published books through the store; and the store itself published more than a dozen titles. However, the Espresso Book Machine was not the game-changing device Epstein had hoped it would be. Within a few years, increasing maintenance costs, involving serious issues that required flying in a mechanic from St. Louis, and the reduction of costs in larger scale on-demand printing programs (such as the one operated by Ingram Books), caused many of the stores to abandon the machines. However, the machine did introduce on-demand printing to stores, and many, including Village Books, continue to aid authors in publishing and maintain a publishing program of their own.

Bookstores' process of buying new book inventory has also evolved over the years. Four decades ago, piles of printed catalogs would arrive in the bookstore. Smaller stores would peruse the catalogs and place orders with publishers or wholesalers by mail or phone. Stores fortunate enough to see publishers' sales representatives would go through the catalog(s) with their rep, who would present information about print runs, marketing plans, sales records of authors' previous books, and other information. The reps would take orders and submit them to the publisher. It was a time-consuming process.

One of the first efforts toward increased ordering efficiency came in the late 1980s from Random House. Sales representatives went through the season's catalogs before their sales calls and sent a list of suggested order numbers to each store: five copies of Title A, three copies of Title B, ten copies of Title C, and so on. Though there was still a discussion of pertinent information regarding the books and authors, it allowed a store to see where the publisher's emphasis was for the season and gave buyers an opportunity to think about each of the suggested books and potential order numbers ahead of time.

Further improvements in the ordering process followed. Shortly after the turn of the century, John Rubin noticed the difficulties experienced by his mother Roberta Rubin in running her independent bookstore, The Book Stall in Winnetka, Illinois. To help her out, he created a bookstore analytics program. The program worked so well that John rolled it out as Above the Treeline in 2004. The industry newsletter Shelf Awareness reported in their January 30, 2006, issue that it was the hot new product at that year's Winter Institute. The program allowed booksellers to see how their own sales of individual titles compared to other stores and to find titles others were selling well that they might not be stocking.

In 2008, Above the Treeline launched Edelweiss, a digital catalog service that offered electronic versions of catalogs from eight publishers. By 2013, every major publisher had their catalog on Edelweiss. Like the system Random House had launched, Edelweiss allows a sales representative to individually, digitally mark up catalogs for each store. Store buyers can view those marked-up catalogs and make buying decisions. The program has reduced the amount of time spent talking about the books and shifted the reps' role to helping to plan display and marketing of the titles.

Fairness and Freedom: Social Issues in the Book Business

Attempting to create a level playing field in the bookselling business has been a constant struggle throughout the history of U.S. bookselling.

With the growth of the chain stores, it became clear that the chains were negotiating special deals that were not available to independent stores. If it could be proved, this would violate the law.

In 1993, while I was president of the ABA, an investigation was launched into publishers' selling policies and practices. With the data in hand, ABA filed suit against five publishers on the first day of the annual ABA convention in 1994. The suit contended that independent booksellers had been disadvantaged by publishers' discriminatory selling practices. In 1995, a court-monitored consent decree was signed, putting publishers on notice that such practices would no longer be tolerated.

The story didn't end there. In 1997, it came to light that Penguin USA had violated the consent decree. A settlement of $25 million dollars was awarded to ABA , which set aside half to be shared with member booksellers. Any ABA member bookseller who could prove they bought at least one Penguin book during a particular period was awarded $1,000. Stores that had records of larger sales claimed many thousands of dollars. Years later, Oren Teicher, former CEO of ABA, looked back on this event in an April, 2022 issue of *Publishers Weekly*:

I think the ABA litigation contributed to raising the consciousness of antitrust matters in the book business and helped lay the groundwork for the indie resurgence. Inequalities still exist for sure, most notably these days with Amazon. In hindsight, [it] was the right thing for us to have done at the time. Having said that, times do change, and I think the more collegial and less adversarial relationship ABA developed with publishers over the past decade has also been appropriate and has worked to the advantage of indie stores.

Like digitization, globalization is another business trend that has affected nearly every segment of the industry, and the book business has not been immune. As I noted earlier, Penguin Random House, owned by German-based Bertelsmann, operates throughout the world. Hachette Book Group, considered an American publisher, is owned by Hachette Livre, a French corporation that is the third largest publisher in the world. The French company La Martinière Groupe owns Abrams Publishing Company. HarperCollins has publishing groups in the United States, Canada, the United Kingdom, Australia, New Zealand, Brazil, India, and China. And bookstores have been touched by globalization as well. Before its demise, Borders Group owned stores in the U.K., Australia, New Zealand, and Singapore. Though Barnes and Noble doesn't operate stores outside of the U.S., its CEO is James Daunt, the owner of six independent London bookshops and managing director of the London-based Waterstones chain. Even independent bookstore Books & Books in Miami once had a partnership with a bookstore in the Cayman Islands.

Finally, no survey of trends in bookselling and publishing would be complete without a discussion of the recent waves of efforts to censor or ban books.

When the American Booksellers Foundation for Free Expression (ABFFE) was formed in 1990, those of us on the board would have thought that, by the 2020s, we would have eliminated censorship or, at least, reduced its impact. We won a lot of battles over the intervening years. But now, more than thirty years later, we have once again seen a gigantic surge in the attack on books, this time with a coordinated effort unlike any we've seen in the past.

It's impossible to think about the battle against censorship and for reader privacy without thinking of Joyce Meskis, who, though she disliked being called a hero of the First Amendment and reader privacy, richly deserved the moniker. Joyce fought censorship over and over again in her home state of Colorado, including appealing a case to the Colorado Supreme Court (against her attorney's advice) that ultimately led to a decision that changed the law and protected reader privacy. She chaired the task force that led to the founding of ABFFE and testified before the Senate Judiciary committee in opposition to the Pornography Victims Compensation Act. In recognition of these and other efforts, in 1995 she received the PEN/Newman's Own First Amendment Award—and then used the $25,000 prize to establish the Colorado Freedom of Expression Foundation.

PLUS ÇA CHANGE, plus c'est la même chose. Does the French saying really apply to the business of books ? It might seem as though the last forty years have been a time when everything has changed in the industry.

But I would argue that some important, fundamental truths about the publishing and bookselling world remain much the same as ever. Most important, I would say that people in the business—both publishers and booksellers—are still passionate about the written word and love putting books, in whatever format, in people's hands. While the path of the book may have added some new links over the years, the chain from writer to reader remains unbroken. Publishing and bookselling are ancient professions, and though technology, consolidation, globalization, and other trends may have changed how each step is accomplished, the result remains the same—connecting people and ideas. May it always be so.

9.
Catalyzing a Revolution in Book Marketing

Carl Lennertz

Carl Lennertz has held executive positions at several publishing houses and nonprofits. He was VP of Marketing at Knopf for 10 years and held marketing positions at HarperCollins and Little, Brown. He organized over 2,000 national author tours and oversaw bestselling book campaigns as well as debut launches. He published a book with Random House and has edited over twenty-five books. Lennertz taught marketing at the University of Denver for eleven years. His nonprofit and association work includes the American Booksellers Association (working on a national campaign for independent bookstores), World Book Night US (where 250,000 free books were handed out to people in need each year on April 23), and now as the executive director of the Children's Book Council and Every Child a Reader for six years. He has lived in upstate New York's Adirondacks since 2019.

bell·weth·er (noun) - one that takes the lead or initiative; a person or thing that assumes the leadership or forefront, as of a profession or industry. Also: an indicator of trends. Synonyms: *leader, pacesetter, trailblazer*

T HE WORD *BELLWETHER* entered the lingo at Knopf in the 1980s as the term for all the independent booksellers who were leading the way in discoverability and diversity, long before those words became *au courant*. It also stood for the firsto-week sales figures that were the early indication of whether all the sales and marketing work of the year before the release of a debut novel or important work of history were possibly, maybe, dear god yes about to pay off in terms of that book's success, that author's career, and that season's list in general. We have a spark, sparks!

Joyce Meskis probably never used the word *bellwether* about herself. And likely not *leader*. She was too modest. But she was a leader by example, a trailblazer, and the people she hired at the Tattered Cover, and the many independent booksellers across the country that she mentored, were the catalysts in a revolution in how book marketing was conducted at U.S. publishing houses in the 1980s, 1990s, and to this day.

The impact of the author tour, the bookseller as reviewer, the power of one voice, and the importance of regionality were game-changers in book marketing, and they continue to be just a few of Joyce's many legacies.

She was also ahead of her time as an independent business owner helping to shape how big-city downtowns were perceived, as a champion of the Buy Local movement, as a figure in local politics and on national hot button topics, notably in defense of the First Amendment, and, of course, as a leader in the growth of women-owned and women-led businesses.

Others in this volume can speak to those accomplishments. I will speak to why five—yes, just five—copies of a new book sold in the first week at Tattered Cover, and four or five copies each sold at four or five other bellwether indies the first week, laid the foundation for how books were marketed for decades to come.

Let's look back at the bookselling and publishing marketing land-scape just before Joyce opened the first Tattered Cover in 1974 so we can see how much has changed. Coming out of the 1960s, the bookstore world was dominated by 1,200 Walden and 800 B. Dalton mall stores. The book review media was dominated by big city print and national print, TV, and radio. The world was top-down and homogenous. There's a reason that the books up front in most mall stores were called *mass market.* (I started out at Waldenbooks, and job one each day was refilling the up-front floor displays (painfully referred to as *dumps*) of mass market paperbacks, but always taking two or three copies back out so it looked like there was activity.)

Publishing companies at that time didn't even have positions with the word "marketing" in them. Sales and publicity staff oversaw book promotion, and marketing plans with independent bookstores at the center of those plans were non-existent. A big-book marketing plan was pretty cookie cutter: big-city reviews, a radio or TV interview, and floor displays and posters. A lot of cardboard. Midlist and debut book plans were all review-reliant.

At Random House, sales reps actually received a Western Union mailgram every other week or so if news of a *Today Show* was breaking, or some other big deal. Later, in the office in the 1980s, I was the one who wrote up those mailgrams, and my assistant would go over to a special machine to type up news of an Oprah appearance or a *New York Times Book Review* front-page review. (Not-so-ancient history; just an-cient technology.)

I "went to school" at Waldenbooks, as many others in publishing did. B. Dalton Booksellers was also a wellspring of future publishing folks. The store inventories were mostly the same, as they were at the other stores that filled the malls or downtowns of America.

The book world was New York City-centric, as was book promotion, as bestsellerdom often hinged on a major *New York Times* review or a major TV network talk show interview. And beyond NYC, big city department store book departments and large independents dominated the book scene in the top ten cities population-wise. In Chicago, for instance, Kroch's & Brentano's and Marshall Field's department stores ruled the roost. Kroch's depth of inventory was remarkable (though carrying such deep stock, often literally in stacks, would prove to be an Achilles heel when Crown came to town in the 1990s). Students of bookselling are familiar with the names of the other flagship department stores who were so important that the buyers of each were feted in some fashion at every American Booksellers Association (ABA) show. In addition to Marshall Fields, there was Macy's, Kaufmanns of Pittsburgh, Rich's of Atlanta (book buyer Faith Brunson was a star), Famous-Barr of St. Louis, Hudson's in Detroit, and others. All central to the bookselling scene, and all bestseller-stocked.

HOWEVER, OUT OF THE 1960S AND 1970S came a new generation of booksellers—women and men who would have their individual voices heard, and whose store inventories were personal, varied, and idiosyncratic.

The 1970s was when women college graduates equaled the number of men for the first time, beginning a dramatic and much needed shift in who would be the future booksellers, future editors, *and* the majority of future readers. The male-dominated publisher workplace was also changing, rapidly and thank goodness.

The list of women booksellers who opened or expanded existing stores or became the main buyers in the 1970s and 1980s reads like—

no, is!—a Hall of Fame roster, along with Joyce: Roxanne Coady, Roberta Rubin, Betsy Burton, Gayle Shanks, Anne Christopherson, Carla Cohen, Barbara Meade, Carole Horne, Kris Kleindienst, Dana Brigham, Fran Keilty, Carla Jimenez, Becky Anderson, Suzy Staubach, and many more.

There were the guys, too, of course, including many who would join Joyce as mentors and leaders: Mitchell Kaplan, Paul Yamazaki, Steve Bercu, Rick Simonson, Michael Powell, David Schwartz, David Unowski, John Evans, Britton Trice, and Clark Kepler, to name a few. And the famous couples: Barbara and Ed Morrow, Dee and Chuck Robinson, Maggie and Michael Tucker, and Richard and Lisa Howorth.

Let's pivot to another famous bookseller who illustrates some of Joyce's leadership magic. I speak of Margaret Maupin, the head book buyer who was more the face of Tattered Cover to many of us in publishing than Joyce, who had the confidence and wisdom to put someone else in the limelight.

These names—Joyce, Margaret, Roxanne, Mitchell, and all the others—are important in that we in marketing knew them, either through in-person meetings at shows or by mail—snail mail, no e- yet. And their reputations and influence were such that I just listed first names above because you'll know who I am talking about if you've been part of the book scene. It was so important because we had faces to the names and knowledge of what they liked to read, and we knew that if we sent out twenty-five early galleys to book lovers like these, we'd get more than a dozen enthusiastic endorsements.

And this fact marked a sea change in book marketing across every publishing house: the bookseller as reviewer, advance reader, trendsetter, bellwether.

Indie booksellers would now form the core of many a marketing campaign, and the national TV show or *NYTBR* review would not have to be the make-or-break. Yes, reviews helped, of course, as they sent customers into stores asking for the books, being the push part of the push-pull sales and marketing equation. But there are four things to note here:

- o That if said book wasn't up front due to our advance work, the sales connection in store might not be made;
- o That our advance work and a nice stack up front or a face-out on the "new arrivals" table would get a book moving even if the reviews were slow to come;
- o That advance store staff support would also lead to those ubiquitous and utterly pure and organic handwritten staff picks shelf talkers (which some publishers, hilariously and foolishly, tried to simulate with scripted shelf talkers in sans serif script); and
- o That these were not just individual books being promoted, but author careers launched—because in the indie booksellers we had partners for the long haul.

At the time, you could begin to look at the *Times* bestseller list— still the yardstick back then—and see that, more and more often, the Michael Ondaatjes and Toni Morrisons, Barbara Kingsolvers and Kazuo Ishiguros could all trace their success back to an indie well-spring.

Lest you think I am only talking about literary fiction, there are legendary stories of booksellers who were credited with commercial fiction bestsellers: Mary Gay Shipley and *The Divine Secrets of the Ya-Ya Sisterhood*, Warren Cassell and *The Bridges of Madison County*, and those first five indies that blessedly welcomed in a fella with a self-published legal thriller entitled *The Firm*.

ONCE THE FIRST BOOKSELLER ENDORSEMENTS on a new book arrived, a force multiplier effect kicked in: booksellers would tell each other about their discoveries at the ABA show, at regional shows, and by phone. We marketing folks were amplifiers as well, in letters listing the blurbs from fellow booksellers, or, yes, faxes. (We're still pre-email here.)

Word of mouth was taking on an all-new, layered meaning.

Word of mouth is often thought of as a consumer phenomenon. But before it could even happen, in meetings and in the halls of publishing, word of mouth amongst colleagues was the first spark, and then in the growing world of bellwether indie booksellers, a central part of many a marketing plan was transferring the in-house buzz to the indies, creating another level and meaning of word of mouth that was still pre-consumer.

Then something else happened. Booksellers meeting up at regional or national meetings would share news of how wonderful these authors were—many of them debut writers yet to be on the bestseller lists—and, before long, a five-city author tour turned into a 25-50 city word-of-mouth love fest, and none of them were anchored in New York City. Denver, along with cities like Milwaukee, Portland, Phoenix, and Kansas City, tipped the geographic center of bookselling, if not publishing, to the middle of the country. New York, Boston, and D.C. were still gold for book sales and author events, but the epicenter was moving.

And then, the next impact of Joyce's way of doing things came to the fore. The brilliance of Joyce was putting her booksellers out in front as faces of the store. An advance blurb from Margaret Maupin was gold! And because Margaret couldn't read *everything*, galleys were spread around the store, and we marketing folk began getting return post cards and reports from the reps with blurbs from many different booksellers in many different indies.

This was a paradigm shift—that blurbs from booksellers in Denver, Blytheville, Santa Cruz, St. Paul, or Iowa City would essentially coalesce into a value equal in importance to building a book career as that provided by a review from an esteemed book reviewer.

This meaning of word-of-mouth was *now the* thing, along with its soul mate, hand-selling. (I always thought of those handwritten shelf talkers as hand-selling for us shy folks who don't always want to inter-act in person when shopping. Also, busy booksellers can't be every-where in the store in person, so shelf talkers ensured that they and their personalities and their personal tastes were front and center in their scrawls all over the store.) Talk about being a bellwether: I picked up the mass market chunk of a book called *A Game of Thrones* at Keplers in the mid-1990s thanks to a shelf talker.)

What began as infamously plain galleys with very pale pastel all-type covers—often called Cranes, as they were printed by Crane & Co. on Cape Cod—sent out to gather bookseller quotes a full year ahead of publication, expanded to nicely bound galleys with some actual jacket art to full-out advance reader's copies/editions, or ARCs or AREs de-pending on where you worked. (I always preferred "arc.")

One iteration along that road were much prized "oh booksellers will never read manuscripts" bound manuscripts with a note from the editor or publisher. (Every launch meeting at Knopf included a debate as to which bound manuscript might include a cover note from the ven-erable editor in chief Sonny Mehta.)

Another really cool iteration took place when Random House pro-duced a reader's copy of Richard Russo's *Nobody's Fool* featuring . . . drum roll . . . sales rep endorsements. The reps, after all, were and still are the conduit to and from the indie booksellers and publishing HQs.

And then, coming full circle to indie booksellers as bellwethers, quotes from well-known booksellers who received early galleys went on the covers of the larger round of ARCs/AREs, spreading the fire, that early bookseller word of mouth, far and wide.

Further to Joyce as leader and bellwether, Margaret's name (and later Cathy Langer's) appeared on many of these galleys. And then, in a further sharing of power and agency, the booksellers on the floor or those who managed certain departments began to see their names on reader's copies, in rep reports back to the main office, and more.

I've read that the best leaders create more leaders, and Joyce and her generation certainly did that.

IN A COMPLEMENTARY DEVELOPMENT to the notion of bellwether indies, early galleys, and booksellers as reviewers, the 1980s saw a rise in author tours that frequented independent bookstores way beyond the "I-95 tour followed by a hop over the country to the West Coast" model. Not that there weren't great indies in Boston, New York, D.C., Los Angeles, and San Francisco, but indies in the rest of the country were yearning to be heard and visited.

And what those of us coming up in sales at the time recall most is that while the event itself might not generate a big sales number, the lasting effect of the author's visit to a store had a long-lasting impact on sales of that book and of a career. Name me a bestselling author and chances are good they can trace their first success to a bookseller or two who championed their debut book—and book two, book three, and beyond. Bellwether indies were both advance early supporters and loyal for years to come. (See the document on page 132, "10 Benefits of an Author/Reading Event," which I created years ago for nervous publicists to share with nervous authors. It speaks to the many things indies did and do to support authors.)

10 Benefits of an Author/Reading Event at a Bookstore That Have NOTHING To Do with the Event Itself . . . But Everything To Do with Going to That Store!!

Concerned about a low turnout? Worried about the cost of store events? An understandably upset author if no one shows up, or one or two people? It happens. Bad weather. Local sporting or cultural event. Other national or local news/events.

IT DOESN'T MATTER!! SO MANY GOOD THINGS CAN HAPPEN BY THE AUTHOR'S PRESENCE AT THE STORE. READ ON.

HERE ARE 10 THINGS THAT WOULD **NOT** HAVE HAPPENED HAD THE AUTHOR NOT GONE TO THE STORE FOR A READING IN THE FIRST PLACE:

1. Book display before the event.
2. A biggie: A listing in the store's newsletter/events calendar that gets circulated to hundreds and thousands of book lovers.
3. Raised awareness to local reviewer/media.
4. Noticed by local reading groups.
5. Display after the event.
6. Signed stock for sale after the event.
7. One or two people in attendance? Read your heart out as if it were 100. They will rave to others, and you never know who they might be.

8 & 9. The DOUBLE Biggie: A bookseller in the store, or several, will move your book to the top of their reading stack, ahead of tons of other reading, and that will beget a long life of staff picks and in-store word of mouth, which begets sales!

10 Lastly: **ALL OF THESE EVENTS WOULD NOT HAVE HAPPENED HAD THE AUTHOR NOT GONE TO THE STORE FOR A READING IN THE FIRST PLACE.**

I have seen over and over again where books sold 50, 100 copies *after* an event . . . AND an author made a lifelong fan in the store . . . and careers have been made. Just by showing up.

If you don't, someone else will. Enjoy it. Revel in the spontaneity of word-of-mouth. It works.

And it often has to start in person.

Back to those five copies sold the first week at Tattered Cover: it almost feels absurd to look back and think that was really a true measurement. But before the days of supply chain, spreadsheets, and BookScan, at Knopf we built a mini-five-store BookScan, if you will. Each Sunday or Monday morning, in time for the weekly sales meeting on current titles, I'd have faxes in hand with numbers on a dozen key new titles from just a handful of indie stores.

The total number of books sold at all indies couldn't be aggregated into a nice, fat figure to be digested in Monday-morning sales meetings (as the chain numbers could). But just listing those often single-digit first, second, and third numbers gave us a glimpse at what we knew was the tip of the iceberg—and gave us hope.

THE NEXT MAJOR DEVELOPMENT in book marketing came from the fact that the book business is one of the few businesses where people share—give away!—their best business practices. From introducing sidelines, coffee counters, going off-site for events, and more, booksellers openly donated their successful ideas to those who were, on the face of it, competitors.

Joyce Meskis and her indie cohort fostered the mindset of a rising tide lifting all boats.

And the most important shared idea of all? Reading groups. It is difficult now to fully realize the positive changes this concept brought to the book world: indies as even stronger centers of community; sales increases by a hundred-fold; more attention to paperback marketing (which had previously been an afterthought); more paperbacks with great covers and, in the next iteration, a book club seal on the cover; and most important, an increase in the diversity of the authors writing these books.

Backing up a bit to the dawn of this phenomenon, I have a personal story to share. I was reviewing the reorders of the week back in the early 1990s at Knopf and Vintage, and I saw that the Book Stall of Winnetka had ordered ten copies of *The Road from Coorain*, a backlist paperback. Huh. So I called Roberta Rubin—I always enjoyed talking with here anyway—to ask if that was a mistake, if the 10 was meant to be a one.

Roberta: "It's for a reading group that meets in the store once a month." (She might have said "book club." I blame the mists of time.)

Me, the idiot: "What's a reading group?"

Roberta: "It's a group of local mothers with college degrees who want to get out of the house and make new friends and read a book together."

If life were like a movie, there would've been a crescendo of dramatic music playing at that moment.

At the next ABA, every seat in a double-size meeting room at the Javits Center in New York was filled with booksellers waiting to hear from Roberta, Barbara Morrow, and Roxanne Coady about this phenomenon called reading groups and how to start them in their stores.

It's a tribute to Joyce that three of her generation discovered and then shared the very-profitable-to-all idea of reading groups with their colleagues.

Fast-forward again: now publishers rushed to produce reading guides with questions for the groups, first as free-standing printed documents and later just as inserts into the backs of the books; they moved up some paperback release dates to less than a year later; they preemptively and somewhat presumptuously designated some books as reading group picks; and finally, they went straight to paperback originals, more and more often.

As for bookstore sales, the local book group picks were behind the counter so those in the groups could come in and get a discount as a book club member. Finally, stores like Kepler's and Politics & Prose just put the books in bulk out on display only to find that more than 50 percent of the sales were to non-book-club members! It turns out that being a local book club pick is as much an imprimatur of quality as a review in the local paper used to be, and that this also appealed to those not inclined to be in the group (see the previous shyness note). With time, the concept grew to include young adult reading groups and with more history, biography, and current events books joining the previously fiction-dominated phenomenon.

Again, the indie bellwethers, leaders, trendsetters.

JOYCE MESKIS AND HER GENERATION fomented a revolution in bookselling, book marketing, and book publishing, bringing with them a greater understanding of other cultures, ways of life, and identities.

We take much of this new world as second nature now, but everything about book marketing changed, from hardcovers for a debut author becoming a platform building for trade paperback success to the author tour phenomenon.

The next generation have continued to trend-set, notably due to social media, something which Joyce would've likely responded to with, "I don't get it, but let's go for it." And she would've given said new generation free rein to try many new things.

Great leaders create new leaders. Activists beget more activism. Entrepreneurial booksellers and bellwethers like Joyce dragged a staid and chauvinist business into what I feel was and still is a Golden Age of bookselling and book marketing, all to the benefit of our society. Books are a glue that we need more of each day, and booksellers of Joyce's generation and the generations who followed are at the forefront of the fight against book bans and for diversity in hiring and publications.

Joyce was a serious person whose focus was on her own business *and* the well-being of other booksellers, of authors and illustrators, of

IO.

Training the Publishers of Tomorrow: The Bookseller as Educator

David R. Godine and Jill Smith

*David R. Godine was born in Cambridge, Massachusetts, and edu-
cated at the Roxbury Latin School, Dartmouth College, and Harvard
University. After a brief stint in the army, he worked for year as a
printing apprentice to Harold McGrath at Leonard Baskin's Gehenna
Press in Northampton. In 1970, he began David R. Godine, Publisher
with a small trust fund and the ambition of producing a list of general
interest; to act as a general trade publisher, not a specialist. He followed that inspired choice for almost fifty years, issuing countless important and well-reviewed books. The company had offices in
Boston's Back Bay and subsequently in other locations in the area, remaining a part of the city's publishing fabric for many years. David
R. Godine retired from publishing in 2019 and was succeeded by Will
Thorndike, who now serves as president of Godine.*

Jill Smith is director of the Denver Publishing Institute (DPI), which was founded in 1976 in affiliation with the University of Denver. It remains one of the nation's foremost professional training programs for aspiring publishers. Smith joined DPI in 2003, bringing to the program her deep knowledge of the curriculum, as well as a diverse background in corporate communications and business management. During her time at the University of Denver, Smith has completed her MBA through the university's Daniels College of Business. She also earned an MFA from the University of Kansas and her undergraduate degree from Skidmore College.

I NTRODUCING WOULD-BE PUBLISHERS to the practices and protocols of the book business has been a continuing challenge for the industry since its inception. Publishing has sometimes been referred to as "an accidental profession." The expression captures the fact that most people who work in the field didn't grow up dreaming of careers in publishing, and very few sought out academic programs that would systematically prepare them for such work. In this respect, publishers are very different from (for example) attorneys, physicians, nurses, engineers, accountants, or computer programmers, all of whom have complete college and graduate school programs and even entire colleges dedicated to their education. As a result, over the decades, the ranks of book publishers have been filled with people from many various backgrounds—writers, teachers, artists, business people, scientists, musicians, lawyers, you name it—who migrated to publishing for a wide range of personal, social, or economic reasons.

As a result, the only trait that unites most of the people who work in publishing is a love of books. This is arguably a commendable attribute: it means that most book publishing firms are staffed by interesting people with varied backgrounds, each contributing some unique knowledge to the shared enterprise—and since books deal with the entire range of human experience, almost everything under the sun ends up being relevant to book publishing. But it also means that most people in publishing start their careers with little or no understanding of how the business works. They learn on the job, which works very well for some, not so well for others—and the mistakes they make during the learning process can be costly to them and to their employers.

To address this challenge, over the past fifty years, a handful of programs have been created to introduce prospective candidates to the mysteries of the publishing profession. For decades, Joyce Meskis was intimately involved with, and ultimately served as the director of, one of the more important of these academic programs, the Denver Publishing Institute (DPI) at the University of Denver. Joyce's role at DPI is another facet of her wide-ranging contributions to the world of books and publishing, one that many people even within our industry know little about.

The oldest academic program dedicated to the field of publishing is probably the Radcliffe Publishing Procedures Course, founded in 1947 by Diggory Venn in Cambridge. The Harvard reputation and Radcliffe campus provided a natural venue for attracting and educating interested (and generally affluent) recent graduates drawn to the profession. The course, which ran for four weeks, was split more or less equally between book publishing and magazine publishing, arguably two very different industries but ones that attracted the same kind of applicants.

Industry changes sparked by large corporations buying up privately held publishing companies in the 1970s, prompted the Association of American Publishers (AAP) to establish the Education for Publishing Program (EPP), which set out to define the job descriptions and process of book publishing. The EPP sought to connect educators with publishing industry professionals who could supply practical guidance for curriculum development. The momentum generated by this effort helped spark the creation of a number of publishing courses around the country, including the Denver Publishing Institute (1976), NYU's Summer Publishing Institute (1978), the Stanford Publishing Course (1978), and the Pace MS in Publishing Program (1985).*

In 2000, Radcliffe (which by then had been absorbed by Harvard) abandoned its publishing program. It was adopted by Columbia University, where it was managed by Lindy Hess, who had worked for Alfred A. Knopf before rising to become editorial director of Dolphin Books, a division of Doubleday. Hess maintained the traditional dual focus on books and magazines while adding a new "boot camp" element to the program, with students forming mock publishing companies to try out the skills they were learning. Along with a similar program at NYU, the Columbia program continues to this day. Another program was initiated at Stanford University by Della van Heyst, an "intrapreneur" who created a range of executive education programs for the university. The Stanford program concentrated mainly on young mid-career employees already active in the profession and on attracting a strong international cohort. When Stanford closed the program, it was reopened at Yale University under the direction of Tina Weiner, who had risen through the ranks at Yale University Press from sales rep to director (along the way becoming reputedly the first woman at the company to wears pants to work). The program survived at Yale for ten years before being moved to NYU. Bob Baensch, an old publishing hand who'd begun his career with McGraw-Hill in the 1960s and become a dedicated supporter of professional education, was instrumental in all three programs.

Today, a few colleges and universities offer full degree courses in publishing. For example, in Boston, Emerson College has offered an MA degree in publishing and writing under the direction of David

---

* Geiser, Elizabeth A. "Education for publishing in the United States," *LOGOS* 18/1, 2007.

Emblidge, a journalist, author, and publisher. Portland State University offers a masters in publishing in which students publish books under the masthead of Ooligan Press. George Washington University, Pace University, and NYU offer master's degrees in publishing that can be stacked onto their publishing certificate programs. But these extended programs are always under fire for their career outcomes and are economically challenging for the students.

In the mid-seventies, the veteran publisher Fred Praeger (best known for a distinguished line of art books), having sold his company to William B. Benton, publisher and chairman of the Encyclopedia Britannica, moved his operations to Boulder, Colorado, and started a new company, Westview Publishing. In the process of the sale, he had developed a friendship with the president of the Encyclopedia Britannica, Maurice Mitchell, who had left the company and New York to become the chancellor of the University of Denver (DU). Praeger and Mitchell looked at the current state of publishing education and recognized the need for a new program, one that would serve the needs of the Midwest and the West, would concentrate exclusively on book publishing, and would attract and enroll a broader spectrum of students than the more elitist Radcliffe/Columbia program.

They worked together to design the curriculum for this new publishing program under the umbrella of DU's School of Library Science, and enlisted Elizabeth Geiser as its first director. Geiser was serving on the AAP's EPP committee and ensconced in New York as the vice president of marketing for Gale Research, a publisher of scholarly and reference works and databases. When she approached her employer at Gale, Fred Ruffner, to determine his support for her new initiative, his response was a generous invitation: "Elizabeth, write your own ticket." And so she did. Geiser launched the Denver Publishing Institute (DPI) in 1976, continuing her job in New York while moving to Denver every summer to lead the program. It was housed within the DU School of Librarianship and led by founding directors Fred Praeger, Maurice

Mitchell, and Elizabeth Geiser. Speakers for that first class included Sam Vaughan, the president of Doubleday, and Peter Mayer, president of Avon books. Elizabeth Geiser ran DPI for thirty-two years.

Joyce Meskis became involved with the program in 1986, lecturing on the business of the bookstore and offering her stores to host DPI events. She served on its faculty for years, bringing to it her steady and unflappable disposition, her unswerving belief in the importance and the central role of books in our society, and her love for "the magic of the reader and the writer coming together."* Of course, she also provided the students with the invaluable perspective of a brilliant bookseller. Some DPI students come to the program with experience as booksellers, perhaps from a part-time job during college. But most lack that experience, which means they've never learned the art of looking at books from the perspective of a bookstore customer—a vital skill that everyone in publishing needs to master. As someone who dedicated her life to connecting books with readers, and had done so successfully countless times, Joyce was the ideal exemplar of that art.

Joyce took over as DPI's director in 2008. She continued to maintain the program's focus on books, realizing that the business models for the magazines and book industries were quite different, as were their modus operandi. DPI differed in other equally significant ways from other programs. The student body was more diverse—geographically, socially, and economically. The Radcliffe/Columbia course tended to attract students from the East, many of them from Ivy League or other well-endowed colleges. By contrast, the DU population was drawn more from state universities and smaller colleges, more widely dispersed and socially diverse. The classes generally included between 90 and 100 students. The speakers were drawn from a wide variety of publishing organizations, including major New York houses, small

---

* Porter, William. "Meet Joyce Meskis: city's literary lioness," *Denver Post*, May 27, 2012.

university and regional presses, and publishers that concentrated in various specialties or were affiliated with specific and widely varied interest groups.

The goals and interests of the students at DPI were equally diverse. Some chose the program because they wanted to spend their summer in the shadow of the Rockies, others because they were unsure of which branch of the industry they wished to enter; still others were specifically interested in design, editing, publicity, or marketing (though many found their interests evolving during the program as they were exposed to facets of the industry they'd never heard about). It was a rich brew, as one of the authors of this essay (David) came to discover. Every summer, David participated in the program during a special day dedicated to the workings of independent presses. This gave him the chance to work closely with a group of students who'd chosen to become "publishers for a day" under his guidance. He would divide the class into several teams, each of which would choose a topic and a title, and use these as the basis for creating an editorial and marketing plan for a book of their own invention. David found he could never anticipate or fail to be astonished by what weird and unexpected expertise would emerge—another illustration of the value of diversity in a publishing organization.

The expert speakers who traveled to Denver to address the students were certainly the drivers of the DPI experience. Joyce knew most of them personally and chose all of them carefully. Her net was all-encompassing. Drawn from all sectors of the industry, they represented the broadest possible range of interests and expertise. About a third came from the major houses in Boston and New York, a third from the rest of the country, and a third from Colorado. The aim was to diffuse the focus, demonstrating that all kinds of publishing were possible and that great publishing could be accomplished anywhere. A small and representative (but hardly exhaustive) sample of the men and women who shaped the industry and were snared by Joyce's net would include

Peter Workman (founder of the independent publisher bearing his name), George Gibson (currently with Grove Atlantic), Jack Jensen (Chronicle Books), Gary Groth (comic book maven and co-founder of Fantagraphics Books), the late Carolyn Reidy (president and CEO of Simon & Schuster), Michael Pietsch (CEO of Hachette), Madeleine McIntosh (then with Penguin Random House), and Sanyu Dillon (now president of the Random House Publishing Group). Other speakers offered focused presentations on a range of specialized topics, from children's books to religious publishing, publicity to design. The speakers were treated as honored guests, put up at a local hotel, fed in the DU dining hall, and occasionally entertained by Joyce and her husband Jed with elegant meals at their downtown LoDo loft.

Jill Smith, a Skidmore graduate, was hired by Elizabeth Geiser in 2003. There was an instant affinity between the two, and when Elizabeth decided to retire and Joyce took over, the same affectionate relationship spilled over into the new regime. Jill's role as associate director of DPI combined two of her favorite worlds—books and academia—and Joyce was careful to introduce her to her network of colleagues and friends, taking her to Book Expo in New York and involving her in curricula and personnel decisions. In 2014, when health reasons suggested that Joyce retire and Jill was tabbed as her successor, her years of mentoring insured that the transition was smooth and seamless. The words Joyce used when commenting about the legacy of her bookstore, would be echoed in her wish for DPI: "One hopes it carries forward, playing some small part in making a better world."[*]

The publishing landscape that Jill now faces as director of DPI has already changed from the one Joyce departed. The changing retail market, the emergence of online services, the evolution of new book formats, the challenges of digital editing, data mining, and metadata have necessitated new foci and topics for the program's curriculum. As one

---

[*] *Ibid.*

example, the world of publishing has been slow to acknowledge that more attention needs to be focused on diversity and a broader representation of a community that a traditionally elitist publishing business has neglected. The DU program, in both theory and practice, has led the charge on this front. However, the core values on which the program was founded, and which Joyce championed during her tenure, remain intact: the belief that books are vital and enduring cultural artifacts and that the people who produce them need to be informed and representative of society as a whole; the creation of a structured training program that can broaden the pool of incoming professionals passionate about books; and the need for a place that welcomed a new generation of aspiring publishers an overview of an industry in which anyone who loved books could find a place and make a difference.

After retiring as DPI director, Joyce remained an active part of the program. She continued to lecture on the business of the bookstore, hosted an annual dinner for the independent publishers' panel, and served as as advisor. Her legacy lives on, not only in the continued survival of the institute she was instrumental in nurturing, but in the countless students who have gone on to careers in publishing, carrying with them the ideals that she embodied as a person and sustaining the legacy and atmosphere she was in instrumental in creating at DPI.

PART THREE

Fights Worth Fighting:
Defending Our Freedom to Read

II.

Judging a Book

Joyce Meskis

Originally published in the Denver Law Review *in January 2002, this essay is Joyce Meskis's first-hand account of the case (*Tattered Cover v. Thornton*) that helped establish the principle that law enforcement officials cannot claim the right to examine the sales records of a bookstore or its customers without a compelling reason. As Joyce noted, giving the government access to information about the books purchased by a particular reader would likely have a "chilling effect" on the free exchange of information and ideas, thereby undermining the First Amendment rights that are fundamental to American democracy. (For a further discussion of this case in the broader context of First Amendment law, see Chris Finan's essay elsewhere in this book.) Joyce's account of the case is fascinating not just for its historical importance but as a vivid illustration of how she thought, analyzed issues, made decisions, and defended her positions—all with extraordinary clarity, firmness, intelligence, and wisdom.*

O N MARCH 17, 2000, the Tattered Cover Book Store received a "subpena" [*sic*] from the Drug Enforcement Agency ("DEA"). The "subpena" required that the Tattered Cover turn over the purchase records of one of the store's customers. Specifically, it asked for the record relating to a mail order purchase, in addition to all other transactions by this particular customer.

I immediately faxed the "subpoena" to our attorney, Dan Recht, who informed me that it was an unenforceable administrative subpoena. We discussed the First Amendment implications of this request. Dan said he would call the DEA agent. Dan informed the agent of our First Amendment concerns and stated that the Tattered Cover would not turn over the information based on this administrative request. He invited the agent to obtain a real subpoena that we would then litigate. The agent indicated to Dan that he did not want to do so, and Dan was left with the impression they were going to let it drop.

We thought the matter was over. However, early in April Dan received a call from Fran Wasserman at the Adams County District Attorney's office. Mr. Wasserman told Dan that a search warrant was being sought in order to obtain the information that the DEA "subpena" had requested from the Tattered Cover. Dan felt that Mr. Wasserman hoped to avoid the search warrant by getting Dan's permission to obtain the information. Dan asked if he could have until the end of the next business day before any action was taken to give him time to contact his client. Mr. Wasserman agreed.

I was incredulous when Dan called to tell me about his conversation with Mr. Wasserman. A search warrant! No opportunity for further judicial review! We agreed to mull over the situation and discuss it the following day.

However, before we had an opportunity to have that conversation, there were four law enforcement officers (soon to be joined by a fifth) in my office, search warrant in hand. I could not believe it! I raised the First Amendment issues, talked about the *Kramerbooks* case, which

put a greater burden on authorities when it came to searches and sei-
zures of constitutionally protected material, all to no avail. The officers
allowed me to contact Dan, who persuaded them to hold off on the execution of the warrant for a week after a series of conversations with
the officers and Mr. Allen, in the Denver District Attorney's office, who
had signed off on the warrant.

The search warrant had been narrowed somewhat from the original request. It required the Tattered Cover to turn over detailed information concerning the mail order shipment, plus all transactional
information relating to that same customer during a one-month period.

We filed for and received a temporary restraining order halting
the execution of the search warrant. This allowed us to litigate the subpoena in the Denver District Court. That case was heard in October
2000, and the judgment rendered half a loaf to each side. Judge J. Ste-
phen Phillips denied authorities (the North Metro Drug Task Force) access to our customer's purchase records over the one-month period.
However, the judge ordered the Tattered Cover to provide the information regarding the specific mail order shipment it had contained.

The facts leading up to the search warrant unfolded over time. Apparently, late in 1999 and early in 2000, the North Metro Drug Task
Force was investigating a suspected methamphetamine lab in a trailer
home in Adams County. During the course of that investigation, they
sifted through the trash outside of the home. In so doing, they found
the leavings of a meth lab as well as an empty mailing envelope with a
Tattered Cover mailing label on it addressed to a person living in the
trailer home. That label also had an invoice number printed on it which
could be used to identify the shipment.

The leavings of a meth lab found in the trash gave police probable
cause to obtain a search warrant for the trailer home. In searching the
home, they found a small meth lab in a bedroom. They also found two
new-looking books on the manufacture of methamphetamines. Neither

had Tattered Cover inventory control stickers on them. One was still in a wrapper. Testimony in court also alleged that neither had the appearance of having been read.

The police found that there were as many as five or six individuals living in or frequenting the trailer home. They concentrated on identifying the occupant of the bedroom. A list of suspects emerged, our customer being Suspect A. Suspect A's address book was found in the bedroom, along with other documents with the names of other individuals. A lot of effort went into building the prosecution of this case, but it all came to a screeching halt with the issue of trying to tie the meth books to Suspect A. The police testified that they saw this as a "piece of the puzzle."

However, when Fran Wasserman was approached to sign off on the search warrant in Adams County, he refused to do so. He indicated to the officers that more investigation was needed. He asked them to check the books for fingerprints and told them that they needed to interview the suspects connected with the trailer home. They proceeded to dust the books, found no useful fingerprints. The officers did not do the interviews in compliance with Mr. Wasserman's request. Instead, they sought the search warrant from another jurisdiction—Denver.

I knew very little about the investigation when the police arrived at the Tattered Cover with the search warrant from the Denver County Court. As our conversation unfolded, I asked one of the officers if our customer (Suspect A) had been contacted so that permission could be obtained for me to turn over the information. The officer said that they had not because the suspect was not the sort to give permission. I thought that might indeed be true if those particular books regarding the manufacture of methamphetamine had been sent in the mailer. If they had not, our customer may have given permission for the police to find out what had been in the mailer. In any case, it seemed to me that there was little to lose in asking, and something might be gained. The officer stressed that they just wanted the information regarding the mail order shipment. I asked the officer what would happen if this did not reveal what they expected it to. He replied that they would then take the next step, which I interpreted to mean that they would seek additional records from the Tattered Cover.

The officers made it clear that they were not investigating the Tattered Cover for illegal activity. I was sure that was the case, because the Tattered Cover is a law-abiding business. I tried to make it clear that the Tattered Cover did not intend to stand in the way of a criminal investigation. As an establishment, we are in agreement with authorities that meth labs are a scourge on the community. We support the police in the difficult job they do.

But, for the Tattered Cover, an individual consumer's book purchase has serious First Amendment implications. We also believe that it is incumbent on the police to protect and honor our First Amendment rights. This case requires a balancing of the necessity of the information the government seeks against important constitutional protections.

As the afternoon wore on, I asked one of the officers how having a book in one's possession could play a role in a conviction for illegal activity. He replied that it could be introduced into evidence to establish the suspect's stale of mind. Curiously, months later he would say that the information regarding the book purchase was sought to establish residency in the bedroom (the police had residency in the trailer home established). Why then, did the police only focus on the books about methamphetamines? Were there other books in the bedroom? What would have been the outcome if the Tattered Cover had not sold the meth books to this suspect? Would that have freed Suspect A of suspicion? I did not think that was likely. How important exactly was this "piece of the puzzle?" Was a "compelling need" (a higher standard than probable cause) clearly established? Given all of the evidence, would there still have been a case without the books? Conversely, if the whole case hung on the books, was it a viable case?

Some have asked me why I did not declare victory after the

decision of the District Court. Would turning over this information really impact our freedom to read? I believe it would. Therefore, the Tattered Cover decided to appeal the decision of the District Court. Briefs were submitted to the Colorado Supreme Court and the oral arguments were heard on December 5, 2001. I am writing this at the end of February 2002 as we await the decision of the court.

While the Tattered Cover is not arguing that the first Amendment enjoys absolute protection, it is arguing that there should be and is a higher standard of protection. It is, after all, one of the very most important pillars of our government. In the *Kramerbooks* case, a District of Columbia District Court Judge ruled that Kenneth Starr, in his subpoena of Monica Lewinsky's book purchase records, could not have unfettered access to such information in his investigation of President Clinton's activities. She ruled that he must demonstrate a compelling need for the information as it relates to such an investigation, which is a higher standard than probable cause. That case never made it to the next step in the judicial process because Ms. Lewinsky struck a deal with Mr. Starr and voluntarily turned over the records.

The Tattered Cover, in its case, urged the court to apply the compelling need standard. We argued that the government did not demonstrate a compelling need for the information to make their case, nor did authorities exhaust their other alternatives in gathering information. Only when there is compelling need and there are no other alternatives should First Amendment guarantees be set aside.

The government argued that the information sought was only a business record, that they could not care less what the suspect read, and that it could be used to establish a state of mind. They contended that a book purchase is no different than a hardware purchase record when it comes to a criminal investigation. I fundamentally disagree.

Entering books into evidence that are found at a crime scene is one thing. Seeking out who bought what from a bookstore is another.

Purchasing, borrowing or "reading a book is not a crime." To edge closer to using a customer's book purchase records as an acceptable way of determining criminal behavior is disquieting at best, and downright frightening at worst. Whether as a reporter seeking information, an iconoclast harmlessly pushing the envelope of societal acceptance, or even someone potentially contemplating illegal behavior, reading is not a crime.

The Tattered Cover is appreciative of the thoughtful consideration Judge Phillips gave to his decision. While we are in disagreement with part of that decision, we could not agree more with the chilling effect that he addressed when speech is thwarted.

Judge Phillips stated: "It is clear that the First Amendment of the Constitution protects the right to receive information and ideas, regardless of social worth, and to receive such information without government intrusion or observation." He went on to quote the late Supreme Court Justice Douglas on the necessity for such protection:

Once the government can demand of a publisher the names of the purchasers of his publications, the free press as we know it disappears. Then the spectre of a government agent will look over the shoulder of everyone who reads. The purchase of a book or pamphlet today may result in a subpoena tomorrow. Fear of criticism goes with every person into the bookstall. The subtle, imponderable pressures of the orthodox lay hold. Some will fear to read what is unpopular, what the powers-that-be dislike. When the light of publicity may reach any student, any teacher, inquiry will be discouraged. The books and pamphlets that are critical of the administration, that preach an unpopular policy in domestic or foreign affairs, that are in disrepute in the orthodox school of thought will be suspect and subject to investigation. The press and its readers will pay a heavy price in harassment. But that will be minor in comparison with the menace of the shadow which government will cast over literature that does not follow the dominant party line. If the lady from Toledo can be required to disclose what she read yesterday and what she will read tomorrow, fear will take the place of freedom in the libraries, bookstores, and homes of the land. Through the harassment of hearings, investigation, reports, and subpoenas government will hold a club over speech and over the press.

When they heard about this case, hundreds of our customers took the time to call or write to us in support of our stand, underscoring this message and raising their own concerns about privacy and the chilling effect on the First Amendment of requiring bookstores to turn over to the police information regarding the purchases of customers.

Editor's note: On April 8, 2002, the Colorado Supreme Court handed down its decision in *Tattered Cover v. Thornton,* finding in favor of Joyce Meskis's bookstore and holding that the search warrant of a bookstore customer's purchase record was unconstitutional.

12.

Fighting for the Freedom to Read, 1923‒2023

Christopher M. Finan

Chris Finan is a writer and historian. For more than 40 years, he led organizations that defend freedom of speech, retiring as executive director of the National Coalition Against Censorship in 2023. A native of Cleveland, Chris is a graduate of Antioch College. After working as a newspaper reporter, he studied American history at Columbia University, where he received his Ph.D. in 1992.

His book, From the Palmer Raids to the PATRIOT Act: A History of the Fight for Free Speech in America *(Beacon Press), won the American Library Association's Eli M. Oboler Award. He is also the author of* How Free Speech Saved Democracy: The Untold History of How the First Amendment Became an Effective Tool for Securing Liberty and Social Justice *(Steerforth Press),* Drunks: An American History *(Beacon Press) and* Alfred E. Smith: The Happy Warrior *(Hill and Wang).*

Chris lives in Brooklyn with his wife, Pat Willard, a writer.

I N MAY 1923, two young Americans, a librarian and a bookseller, independently arrived at a shocking conclusion. At the annual meetings of their professional associations, they declared that librarians and booksellers must fight censorship.

Mary Rothrock, a librarian from Knoxville, Tennessee, told members of the American Library Association (ALA) that it is not the job of a librarian to measure a book's "possible moral effect on mature readers." It is to bring "to all people the books that belong to them."

At the American Booksellers Association convention, an iconoclastic young bookseller from Detroit, Arthur Proctor, told his colleagues that young people wanted books that portrayed life honestly. "They are demanding these books, and so I say that . . . the responsibility of the bookseller towards his customers . . . is not just to sell books that have a sweet ending, but it is their duty to get them the books in spite of the censorship," he said.

Proctor's remarks were so shocking they were stricken from the record.

By some measures, this was the start of the fight for the freedom to read in the United States. Over the course of the next century, there would be many battles, including major conflicts during the McCarthy era and the 1980s. And today the fight continues. In 2023, thousands of books are being pulled from the shelves of schools and libraries.

There has always been censorship in America. Just a few years after the adoption of the First Amendment, which protects freedom of speech and freedom of the press, the Federalists jailed Jeffersonian editors for criticizing President John Adams. By the end of the 19th century, the list of people punished for their speech included abolitionists, suffragists, advocates of sexual freedom, and union organizers.

It was Anthony Comstock, a young Civil War veteran, who created a national censorship regime for the first time in American history. He was not the first to target material with sexual content. But it was Comstock who capitalized on sexual fears by targeting books. "The effect of this cursed business on our youth and society, no pen can describe," Comstock wrote. "All reading and conversation must be of the most pure and elevating character."

In 1872, Comstock went to work as an investigator for the YMCA's Committee for the Suppression of Vice. Only a year later, using the influential connections of his organization and a display of the erotica that he had seized in raids, he persuaded Congress to strengthen the federal obscenity law by making it a crime to mail "obscene or indecent books, papers, articles or things."

He relentlessly pursued men and women who were philosophically opposed to his view of sex. He convicted a doctor for mailing a pamphlet that contained birth control information; an advocate of the view that sexual relations were no business of the government; and a lawyer who protested Comstock's crusade by selling a free love tract that had already been declared obscene. A threat of prosecution forced the pioneering birth control advocate Margaret Sanger to flee abroad.

The publishing community overwhelmingly endorsed Comstock's values. It had long believed that its mission was producing books and magazines that ennobled existence. According to one of the leading American critics of the day, great literature "is that which recognizes the moral conflict as the supreme interest of life, and the message of Christianity as the only real promise of victory."

Nevertheless, a trickle of "bad" books became a torrent in the 1920s. A new generation of authors like Sherwood Anderson, H.L. Mencken, F. Scott Fitzgerald, Sinclair Lewis, John Dos Passos, and Ben Hecht insisted on showing how life was really lived. This included a willingness to deal more frankly with sex. "Let us hesitate no longer to announce that the sensual passions and mysteries are equally sacred with the spiritual mysteries and passions," D.H. Lawrence wrote in 1920.

Many book publishers, authors, librarians, and booksellers were appalled. Arthur Bostwick, the president of the American Library

Association, warned librarians that immigrants were undermining American literature with "standards of propriety [that] are sometimes those of an earlier and grosser age."

Librarians and booksellers sometimes acted as censors themselves. Following Bostwick's call to arms, *Library Journal* asked librarians how they were handling requests for bad books and was flooded with suggestions for ways to thwart dirty-minded readers.

In 1915, Boston booksellers joined with a civic group, the Watch and Ward Society, to review questionable books. Whenever a committee of three booksellers and three Watch and Ward members agreed that a book was unsuitable, they notified all Massachusetts booksellers, who had forty-eight hours to remove it or face possible prosecution.

The fight against a "clean books" bill in the New York legislature in 1923 was a turning point in the attitude of the book industry toward censorship. The National Association of Book Publishers and the American Library Association had both declined to oppose it when it was introduced. But publisher Horace Liveright led a vigorous fight that convinced them of the danger inherent in censorship, and the bill was defeated.

The fight moved next to Boston. In 1927, city officials launched an assault on the new literature. The police chief issued a list of eight novels that he considered obscene, despite the fact that they had all been issued by major publishers and were advertised and sold freely elsewhere. "I have read these books, and I think they are bad," he explained.

Booksellers began pulling titles from their shelves that they feared might subject them to prosecution. They sent the district attorney a case of fifty-seven bestselling titles, requesting an advisory opinion on whether they were obscene. Boston was facing "a sort of moral panic," a reporter for the *New York Times* wrote.

By the spring of 1929, Boston was notorious for its rejection of works that circulated freely in the rest of the country. "Banned in

Boston" had become a national catchphrase, symbolizing narrowness and intolerance.

In the 1930s, librarians continued the fight for the freedom to read. A handful of them convinced ALA to adopt the Library Bill of Rights, which declared that librarians should purchase books based on their "value and interest" and should ignore "the race or nationality or the political or religious views of the writers."

In 1940, ALA created the Intellectual Freedom Committee (IFC) to lead the fight against the American Legion, the Daughters of the American Revolution, and other patriotic groups who were pressuring libraries to purge their collections of "un-American" materials.

The advent of the Cold War following the end of World War II led to a dramatic increase in censorship efforts. In Montclair, New Jersey, the Sons of the American Revolution wanted the library to label and restrict the circulation of all "Communistic or subversive" books and magazines. They also asked the librarian to keep a record of everyone who used the labeled material. ALA took a strong stand against labeling as "an attempt to prejudice the reader, and as such, it is a censor's tool."

But librarians were no match for Senator Joseph McCarthy, who led a campaign to censor government libraries abroad. He claimed that libraries operated by the State Department included books written by un-American authors. The department responded by banning material by "any controversial persons, Communists, fellow travelers, 'et cetera.'"

The threat of McCarthyism convinced ALA to seek support from outside the library community. Over a weekend in early May 1953, twenty-five librarians, book publishers, and citizens "representing the public interest" met at the Westchester Country Club in Rye, New York, to discuss how to halt what the IFC chair called the "national trend toward the restriction of the free trade in ideas."

The result was a statement, *The Freedom to Read*. "The freedom to read is essential to our democracy. It is under attack," it began. "We, as citizens devoted to the use of books and as librarians and publishers responsible for disseminating them, wish to assert the public interest in the preservation of the freedom to read."

The Freedom to Read identified seven propositions: that it was in the public interest for publishers and librarians to make available the widest diversity of views and expressions; that publishers and librarians do not need to endorse every idea or presentation contained in the books they make available; that a book should be judged by its content, not the political views of its author; and that, while obscenity laws must be enforced, it is wrong to limit the efforts of writers to achieve their artistic goals and to deny to adults books that may be unsuitable for adolescents.

Finally, the statement pledged that librarians and publishers, "as guardians of the people's freedom," would "contest encroachments upon that freedom by individuals or groups seeking to impose their own standards or tastes upon the community at large."

"We do not state these propositions in the comfortable belief that what people read is unimportant," the statement concluded. "We believe rather that what people read is deeply important; that ideas can be dangerous; but that the suppression of ideas is fatal to a democratic society. Freedom itself is a dangerous way of life, but it is ours."

The press hailed the release of *The Freedom to Read*. The *New York Times* ranked the statement with "American's outstanding state papers" and joined the *Washington Post*, the *Christian Science Monitor*, and the *Baltimore Sun* in reprinting it in full.

The censors were unimpressed. In 1957, U.S. customs agents seized five hundred copies of *Howl*, a book of poems by Allen Ginsberg. Later, San Francisco police purchased a copy of the book from a clerk at the City Lights Bookstore. They charged both the clerk, Shigeyoshi Murao, and Lawrence Ferlinghetti, the bookstore owner and the publisher of *Howl*, with selling an obscene book.

But things were changing. At that moment, the Supreme Court was deciding the case of *Roth v. United States*, which would determine whether the Comstock obscenity law would continue to determine what Americans could read almost a century later.

Earl Warren, the new chief justice, assigned the majority opinion to another recent appointee to the court, William J. Brennan, Jr. Brennan was not a free speech absolutist. He did not believe that the First Amendment protected obscenity, and he joined five other members of the court in sustaining the conviction of Samuel Roth, the publisher of an explicit magazine.

However, in Brennan's written opinion, he endorsed a narrower definition of obscenity. "... [S]ex and obscenity are not synonymous," he wrote. The First Amendment protected any work with sexual content that is not "utterly without redeeming social importance." While the court had not struck down Comstock's law, it had taken the first step toward protecting artistic freedom.

Conservatives were shocked. In 1961, they struck back against Grove Press publisher Barney Rosset, who had decided it was time for an American edition of Henry Miller's very explicit novel, *Tropic of Cancer*, an underground classic since its publication in Paris in 1934.

Police officials throughout the country began by issuing "unofficial" warnings that the book was obscene. This was sufficient to suppress *Tropic of Cancer* in many places. Frightened wholesalers and retailers returned 600,000 books to Grove. Then the arrests started. Although 2.5 million copies were in print by the end of 1961, it was impossible to buy the book in most parts of the country.

The protest over obscenity reflected a deep anger among many Americans over changes in society. They blamed the media for a loosening of sexual mores.

In 1968, the motion picture industry abandoned decades of self-censorship in favor of a rating system that allowed patrons to decide for themselves how much sex and violence they wanted to see.

Television and radio also began to relax the self-imposed guidelines that restricted content. The TV networks started developing dramas, situation comedies, and soap operas that depicted characters who were divorced, unfaithful, even pregnant and unwed. At the same time, sexually explicit material was increasingly entering the mainstream. Hugh Hefner got the ball rolling in 1953 with the founding of *Playboy* magazine.

In the 1960s, men's magazines were available on newsstands and in drug stores in many parts of the country. "Adult" bookstores sold "hard-core" pornography depicting sex acts, and adult theaters did business in most large cities.

In 1967, members of Congress created the National Commission on Obscenity and Pornography with an expectation that it would demonstrate the harmful effects of sexually explicit material. They were horrified when the commission concluded that such material was not harmful to adults and recommended legalizing it. Members of the Senate repudiated the commission report by a vote of six to five.

President Richard Nixon also condemned the report and began to reshape the Supreme Court. He appointed four justices, giving conservatives control. In 1973, in the case of *Miller v. California*, the Nixon appointees joined in significantly expanding the definition of obscenity. No longer would it be necessary to prove the material was "utterly without social value," although it was still exempt if it had "serious" value.

The court also declared that local communities could apply their own standards in defining obscenity, making it possible for a jury in a conservative city or town to send someone to prison for producing or distributing material that was not illegal elsewhere.

In 1980, the election of President Ronald Reagan gave a powerful boost to the conservative censorship campaign. The first evidence was a sudden jump in the number of challenges to books used in schools and libraries.

More than eight hundred challenges occurred every year in the early 1980s as conservative parents took aim at a wide range of material, including books by Judy Blume and other authors who were writing books for kids that dealt honestly with sex and the other problems they confronted. Books were also attacked for "offensive" language and portraying "antifamily" values.

Meanwhile, antipornography activists pressured the Reagan administration to take strong action against sexually explicit material. Attorney General Edwin Meese appointed a new obscenity commission that was stacked with people who supported vigorous enforcement of the obscenity laws.

Retailers received the message. Without waiting for the commission's final report, the Southland Corporation ordered its 4,500 7-Eleven stores to stop selling *Playboy* and *Penthouse* and recommended that 3,600 franchise stores do the same. Other chains followed suit. Within months, 17,000 stores no longer carried the magazines.

The removal of *Playboy, Penthouse,* and other men's magazines had a domino effect, causing retailers in some parts of the country to drop other controversial magazines, including magazines about rock and roll music, several teen magazines, the swimsuit issue of *Sports Illustrated,* and issues of *American Photographer* and *Cosmopolitan.*

The Justice Department's new National Obscenity Enforcement Unit launched a campaign to destroy the fourteen largest mail-order distributors of sexual material. Justice Department officials made it clear to the owners of these businesses that they must not distribute even non-obscene material like *Playboy* and the popular manual *Joy of Sex.*

Groups like ACLU, the Freedom to Read Foundation, Media Coalition, National Coalition Against Censorship, PEN America, and People for the American Way worked hard to contain the threat posed by the antipornography movement. They testified against bad legislation, filed lawsuits to challenge unconstitutional statues, and undertook a number of important public relations initiatives.

One of the most lasting efforts began in 1982 when the ALA organized the first Banned Books Week, which remains the only national event celebrating the freedom to read. A key element was the creation of displays of banned books, which gave people a chance to see the books that were being attacked. Many were surprised to find some of their favorite books.

The American Booksellers Association (ABA) was particularly aggressive in beefing up its ability to respond to censorship threats. Throughout the 1980s, booksellers had strongly opposed the growing pressure for censorship. In 1986, they joined magazine wholesalers and distributors in founding Americans for Constitutional Freedom to oppose the recommendations of the Meese Commission.

In February 1989, censorship fears reached a new level when Iran's Ayatollah Ruhollah Khomeini issued a *fatwa* calling for the execution of Salman Rushdie, the author of *Satanic Verses*, a novel that many Muslims considered blasphemous. Arsonists bombed a number of bookstores around the world, including two in Berkeley, California.

ABA responded to the crisis by establishing the American Booksellers Foundation for Free Expression. Arts organizations created the National Campaign for Freedom of Expression to oppose efforts by members of Congress to end government grants to controversial artists.

The anticensorship groups depended heavily on volunteers. Throughout the 1980s, publishers, librarians, booksellers, record and video storeowners, writers, artists, and concerned citizens spoke out against censorship. They fought challenges to books in their local libraries, mounted displays during Banned Books Week, and joined in filing briefs to support plaintiffs in important legal cases.

When twelve states passed laws banning the display of material that was "harmful to minors," booksellers became plaintiffs in lawsuits organized by Media Coalition that overturned them. The Supreme

Court ultimately declared that such restrictions violated the rights of older minors as well as adults.

In Michigan, Jim and Mary Dana, owners of a bookstore in a small town, joined the fight after a local church group threatened them with a boycott if they didn't stop selling *Playboy* and *Penthouse*. When state legislators threatened to impose draconian penalties, they organized a state booksellers association that joined with video retailers, magazine distributors, and theater owners in hiring a lobbyist and launching a publicity campaign. The legislation was defeated.

Joyce Meskis was one of the most outspoken booksellers. Just a few years after she opened her then-small bookstore, Tattered Cover, she became a plaintiff in two cases that led the Colorado Supreme Court to strike down a display law and established that the state constitution provided broader protection for speech with sexual content than the First Amendment.

In 1990, when Meskis was elected ABA president, she made it clear that defending the freedom to read would be a priority. "We booksellers are gatekeepers of the expression of ideas," she told ABA members. ". . . [I]t is my view that as booksellers we have our own version of the Hippocratic Oath to maintain the health and wellbeing of the First Amendment."

One of the greatest threats to booksellers at that time was legislation drafted by Catherine MacKinnon and Andrea Dworkin, two feminists who believed that sexually explicit material was mainly responsible for the failure of women to attain social and political equality with men. It authorized civil suits against producers and distributors of "pornography" that purportedly caused sexual violence.

When the Minneapolis City Council adopted a version of the legislation in 1984, it was immediately challenged by ABA, ALA's Freedom to Read Foundation, the Association of American Publishers, and others who feared that it would result in the suppression of mainstream books, magazines, and movies. The law was struck down in a ruling that was upheld by the Supreme Court.

But similar legislation was reintroduced in Congress in 1989 as the Pornography Victims Compensation Act. Meskis and other members of the publishing and entertainment industries testified against the bill in a hearing before the Senate Judiciary Committee. But it was a private conversation, not Meskis's public testimony, that played a critical role in defeating the bill. Meskis visited Senator Hank Brown of Colorado, a Republican member of the committee. His decision to oppose the bill sealed its fate.

With the defeat of the Pornography Victims Compensation Act, it appeared that the culture war over the freedom to publish was largely over. But a real war was about to begin.

In the week after the terror attacks on September 11, 2001, Americans were afraid and angry. They watched the collapse of the World Trade Center endlessly rebroadcast on television. Residents of New York and Washington heard the sounds of fighter jets patrolling overhead. In the subways, soldiers stood guard with automatic weapons. Many Americans wanted to strike back.

Civil libertarians were alarmed. Morton Halperin, a former ACLU official, expressed what was in the minds of many of his colleagues in an email on the day after the attacks. "There can be no doubt that we will hear calls in the next few days for Congress to enact sweeping legislation to deal with terrorism," he wrote. "This will include not only the secrecy provision, but also broad authority to conduct electronic and other surveillance and to investigate political groups."

Halperin's prophecy was swiftly fulfilled by the introduction of a 350-page bill called the USA Patriot Act.

The Patriot Act increased the power of the government to engage in secret searches. Its most chilling provision made it possible for the FBI to seize vast amounts of personal data about American citizens in the dragnet that it was deploying for terrorists. Section 215 authorized the FBI to seek warrants to seize "any tangible things" from businesses, nonprofits, and charities.

While the government had always had the power to issue subpoenas, it normally had to show that there was "probable cause" to believe that a crime has been committed. Under Section 215, however, the government was required to show only that the records were "sought for" a terrorism or espionage investigation. Even worse, Section 215 made no provision for challenging the order in court.

There were expressions of concern about the Patriot Act in both the House and the Senate, but Attorney General John Ashcroft rejected all efforts to amend the bill. Congress overwhelmingly approved it just six weeks after 9/11.

Civil libertarians faced an uphill struggle. The fear of a new attack was strong, and public opinion polls showed overwhelming support for the Bush administration's antiterror policies. One of the major obstacles was the lack of an obvious and imminent threat to civil liberties that was capable of arousing a large number of Americans.

However, the Patriot Act deeply worried two large groups—librarians and booksellers. Both were stunned when they learned that the federal government could use Section 215 to force them to turn over the records of their customers and patrons. They were afraid that people would not feel free to buy or borrow the books they wanted if they knew the government was reading over their shoulder.

Booksellers had gone to court twice in recent years to quash orders to turn over the records of their customers. In 1998, Kenneth Starr, a special prosecutor investigating potential crimes by President Bill Clinton, subpoenaed two Washington bookstores for the purchase records of Monica Lewinsky.

Two years later, five police officers arrived at Tattered Cover with a search warrant and demanded immediate access to the book purchase records of a customer suspected of making illegal supplies of the drug methamphetamine. Meskis called her lawyer, who persuaded the police to withdraw, allowing a judge to decide what information had to be turned over.

It was the beginning of a case that plunged the store and its owner into controversy. Over the next two years, it cost Meskis both time and money. Critics accused her of taking the side of a drug dealer, potentially alienating her customers. She remained resolute. "This is about the right to privacy and the freedom to read what you like without the police looking over your shoulder," she told the *Denver Post*.

When a judge gave her a partial victory, Meskis ignored the advice of her lawyers and appealed the case to the Colorado Supreme Court, seeking a broader ruling. The justices were unanimous in their decision suppressing the search warrant and validating the principle that our freedom to read includes the freedom from government scrutiny of what we read.

In the fall of 2002, just a few months after the decision, the Vermont Library Association sent an open letter to the state's Congressional delegation, urging the repeal of the provisions of Section 215 that threatened reader privacy.

Bernie Sanders, Vermont's sole representative in the House of Representatives, responded by calling a press conference. With a bookseller and a librarian at his side, he announced that he would lead the fight to amend Section 215. "This is a crashing, crushing attack on basic rights in this country, and it's got to be opposed," Sanders said.

ALA, ABA, and PEN America launched a Campaign for Reader Privacy to rally support for the bill introduced by Sanders, the Freedom to Read Protection Act. It started a petition campaign in bookstores and libraries that collected more than 120,000 signatures in its first three months.

In 2005, members of Congress fought over modifying several provisions of the Patriot Act, including Section 215. The final version of a reform bill fell far short of the hopes of civil libertarians. But it did include a number of significant changes. It explicitly recognized that people who receive Section 215 orders have the right to challenge them in court. It also required the director of the FBI to personally authorize all bookstore and library searches under Section 215.

But as history shows, the battle for the freedom to read is never decisively won. A decade later, new threats began to appear.

The political polarization that began in the 1960s had grown even deeper. Black Lives Matter was leading a resurgent movement for civil rights that challenged the idea that racism was a thing of the past.

Once again, young people were in the vanguard of the movement for change, but many of them no longer saw free speech as their ally. Campus activists proposed new measures to protect people of color from hate speech. They asserted that even expressions that are not overtly racist can be harmful. While these "microaggressions" occur throughout society, they called for special care in classrooms and urged professors to provide "trigger warnings" prior to the introduction of content that might be harmful.

A movement to "deplatform" racists by denying them venues in which to present their ideas grew in the wake of demonstrations by white supremacists at the University of Virginia in 2017. By the end of the year, students on various campuses had attempted to block 44 speeches by people they disliked, and more than half of the events had been cancelled.

Pressure to censor was growing in book publishing as well. In some cases, support for more books by people of color became demands for suppression of books deemed supportive of racism. In 2016, critics took aim at *A Fine Dessert*, a picture book for young children that depicted how four families ate the same dessert during different periods of American history, including a mother and daughter who were slaves on a Southern plantation.

Reviewers loved the book, but others thought it was insufficiently critical of slavery. They objected strongly to an image of a young slave smiling. Similar criticism caused Scholastic, the largest publisher of children's books, to take the highly unusual step of withdrawing *A Birthday Cake for George Washington*, which featured the cook who was one of the president's slaves.

Some of the protests came from within the publishing houses. Staff members began questioning whether their employers should be releasing books by conservative authors and men accused of sexual abuse. When Hachette announced plans to publish an autobiography by filmmaker Woody Allen in the wake of accusations that he'd molested his stepdaughter, dozens of its employees staged a walkout, causing the cancellation of the book. (It was later published by Arcade Publishing, an imprint of the independent publisher Skyhorse.)

Several months later, during the first weeks of the protest over the murder of George Floyd, five publishing employees urged other staff members not to work during a "Day of Action" to show their support for Black Lives Matter and to demand greater diversity in the industry.

"We are disrupting and taking action by refusing to participate in a system complicit with white supremacy and racial capitalism for a day," they explained in a statement signed by 1,300 people. One of their goals was to "pressure publishers to stop publishing racist books."

By the middle of 2020, liberals who sympathized with the goals of the new protest movement were beginning to express concern about the impact of deplatforming and other expressions of intolerance on the publishing industry and American culture generally.

A letter published in *Harper's Magazine* over the signatures of 153 prominent writers, journalists, and academics declared, "The free exchange of information and ideas, the lifeblood of a liberal society, is daily become more constricted." It condemned "an intolerance of opposing views, a vogue for public shaming and ostracism, and the tendency to dissolve complex policy issues in blinding moral certainty."

A year later, the political situation changed profoundly when conservatives launched another censorship crusade. During a race for governor of Virginia, the Republican candidate Glenn Youngkin made an issue of the fact that Toni Morrison's novel, *Beloved*, was being taught to high school students without the permission of their parents. A campaign ad attacked his opponent for vetoing a bill that gave parents more control over what their children could read. Youngkin won.

Conservative activists quickly concluded that censorship could be a winning issue. School board meetings had become battlegrounds during the Covid-19 pandemic as parents expressed their anger over school closures. Republican politicians fed the flames by claiming that kids were being exposed to pornography and brainwashed by Critical Race Theory in public schools.

Book banning had eased considerably since the 1980s. Most school districts had adopted formal procedures for handling challenges. When a book was challenged, a committee was appointed to review it. Composed of educators, a parent, and sometimes a student, these reconsideration committees read the book and usually voted to retain it. The number of challenges fell to 156 in 2020, according to ALA.

The number skyrocketed in 2021. There were 729 challenges to 1,529 different titles. There were almost twice as many the following year—1,269 challenges to 2,571 titles. The vast majority of the books were written about members of the LGBTQ community and people of color.

The avalanche of challenges overwhelmed school boards. In many cases, they abandoned reconsideration policies that required books remain available on the shelves while they were being reviewed. Some districts pulled dozens of books simultaneously, making it unlikely they would ever be returned.

The book banners were becoming more organized. Two Florida women launched Moms for Liberty, which quickly grew into a national organization that claimed 120,000 members. It took credit for electing over two hundred school board members in its initial campaign.

Anticensorship groups struggled to respond to the massive attack. In December 2021, the National Coalition Against Censorship sought to rally support for the fight by issuing a statement that was endorsed by more than six hundred non-profit organizations, businesses and individuals. Its Kids Right to Read Project wrote to school boards across the country to protest violations of their reconsideration policies.

In the summer of 2022, ALA launched Unite Against Book Bans, a campaign to identify supporters at the local level. NCAC began organizing a Kids' Right to Read Network to support local anticensorship groups and help launch new ones.

In June 2023, the publishing community joined ALA and others in reaffirming its commitment to the freedom to read by celebrating the 70th anniversary of *The Freedom to Read*. Their statement quoted from the original. "The freedom to read is essential to our democracy. It is constantly under attack," it said.

The anniversary was a reminder that, 100 years after it started, the fight for the freedom to read continues.

13.

The Library, the Marketplace, and the Endless Buffet: Rethinking the Governing Metaphor for "The Freedom of Speech"

Steven D. Zansberg

Steve Zansberg is a First Amendment lawyer in Denver, Colorado. He defends news organizations, reporters, authors, publishers, and other information providers against claims actually filed or threatened based on content, and he provides prepublication review to reduce the risk of such claims being filed. He also serves as the president of the Colorado Freedom of Information Coalition, a not-for-profit educa-tion group devoted to increasing transparency in Colorado's state and local government operations. (Joyce Meskis was an active member of the CFOIC's Board, and was the 2000 recipient of that organization's prestigious Jean Otto Award for her sustained commitment to the free flow of information to the public.) Steve also authored the amicus brief to the Colorado Supreme Court in the Tattered Cover v. City of Thornton *case, on behalf of American Booksellers Foundation for Free Expression, the American Library Association, Freedom to Read Foundation, the Association of American Publishers, and others.*

"Congress shall make no law . . . abridging the freedom of speech or of the press . . ."

I NSIDE AN ACTUAL (PHYSICAL) BOOKSTORE or library, one can wander among shelves of books and periodicals—and, in more recent times, CDs, DVDs, and multiple other form of media—and be exposed to ideas and thoughts one may not have even considered perusing when one entered the store. It is that sense of unlimited possibilities, the serendipitous discovery of new horizons and uncharted adventures, that we experience when we enter a bookstore or library. Crossing that threshold can be likened to standing with one foot on the ground and the other on a ship, airplane, or randomized time machine, about to embark on a new journey, destination completely unknown.

These comparisons are metaphors—linguistic constructs by which we compare our real, lived experience at a particular time and place to an abstract symbol that "stands for" or captures that thing's essential characteristics, and thereby illuminates a broader concept, proposition, or idea.* So allow me, in this brief essay, to suggest that the bookstore (and/or library) stands for much more than what it may appear to be

---

* For an insightful examination of the role that metaphors play in First Amendment jurisprudence, see Robert L. Tsai, *Fire, Metaphor, and Constitutional Myth-Making,* 93 Georgetown L. J. 181 (2004); George Lakoff & Mark Johnson, *Metaphors We Live By* (Chicago: University of Chicago Press, 1980); *see also infra* note 17.

on the surface.[†] To the naked eye, the bookstore is a physical repository of different forms of written communications. It is also a place of commerce, where consumer goods are bought and sold, often including trinkets, greeting cards, and various novelties, available alongside the collection of written works.

But beyond its mundane physical attributes, the bookstore is so much more.

The bookstore is, dare I say it, the embodiment of what the First Amendment means when it declares that Congress (and by judicial extension, all forms of governmental authority) is prohibited from infringing "the freedom of speech." That freedom is enshrined in our Constitution alongside our freedoms, as individuals, to believe in whatever religion we choose, or none at all; to gather ("assemble") with others holding similar beliefs—*ideas* and *thoughts* that cannot be proven true or false; and to collectively bring our "grievances" to the attention of our public servants, those chosen by our votes to represent "We the People."

There is a reason that all of these seemingly disparate freedoms are collected together in a single amendment to the Constitution: they all embrace individual autonomy and the freedom of thought—the freedom from official coercion to share the view of any ordained orthodoxy, be it religious, social, moral, or even scientific/data-based in origin.

[†] Although this essay uses the two interchangeably, the United States Supreme Court has formally recognized the exploratory, horizon-expanding nature of a public school library. *See Bd. of Educ., Island Trees Union Free Sch. Dist. No. 26, Et Al. v. Pico*, 457 U.S. 853, 869 (1982) ("A school library, no less than any other public library, is a place dedicated to quiet, to knowledge, and to beauty. . . . [I]n the school library[,] a student can literally explore the unknown, and discover areas of interest and thought not covered by the prescribed curriculum. . . . Th[e] student learns that a library is a place to test or expand upon ideas presented to him, in or out of the classroom.").

Men (people, more broadly) in our new nation, were guaranteed the fundamental right to think and believe whatever they chose to. Bad acts—conduct causing harm to other individuals or to "the public welfare"—could be appropriately sanctioned and even prohibited prospectively. But no person could be punished in any way for harboring bad thoughts.

As we shall see, this foundational concept of individual liberty—freedom of choice, freedom of thought—has been embraced by the Supreme Court in interpreting the First Amendment throughout our history. And our freedom to decide which ideas we will embrace and which we will reject explains why the bookstore or library, properly considered, is an appropriate metaphor for the freedom of speech enshrined in our First Amendment. But, in my view, it is too literal a symbol to serve as a sufficiently abstract descriptor of the freedom to think independently, free from government interference.

Instead, I will suggest that the bookstore/library—access to unlimited sources of information—is a useful stepping stone to arrive at a fuller, grander metaphor: an endless buffet of food for thought.

The Freedom to Receive Information

On its face, the First Amendment's so-called "free speech clause" speaks only of the rights of the speaker, whether the "speech" be communicated orally (the speaker standing on the proverbial soapbox in the town square or park), in writing (whether it be the "lonely pamphleteer" or "the press"), or through myriad other forms of expression, including motion pictures, painting, sculpture, dance (expressive conduct), clothing/fashion (a T-shirt emblazoned with a slogan), a burning cross, a swastika, or, in modern times, a series of digitized zeros and ones. And, no doubt, that clause does protect the rights of those who generate and disseminate ideas and messages. For outside of certain clearly and narrowly defined areas of "unprotected speech" such as "true threats," "obscenity," "fighting words," and "defamation,"—all circumscribed by well-demarcated boundary lines established through many decades of litigation and jurisprudence—the government may not abridge the freedom of anyone disseminating ideas in these and many other forms.

But that freedom belongs as well to the audience to whom the speakers' messages and ideas are directed. After all, from the speaker's perspective, the "freedom to speak" only inside an empty closet or alone in a remote cave is, in actuality, no freedom at all.* The freedom to *receive* the speaker's message explains why the free speech clause is deliberately set forth alongside the other rights enshrined in the First Amendment, all of which guard against government interference with individuals' freedom to *think* independently and to decide for himself or herself what to *believe*. Not only is there a so-called "free exercise clause" that protects the freedom to embrace and practice one's own religion, there is also the "no establishment clause" that provides a freedom *from* religion, a categorical prohibition on the government ordaining any set of beliefs that must be adopted by all or even some of the people. The First Amendment forbids any form of government-imposed "orthodoxy" of thought, be it religious, political, scientific, or "factual."†

---

* See, e.g., Lamont v. Postmaster Gen., 381 U.S. 301, 308 (1965) (Brennan, J., concurring) ("The dissemination of ideas can accomplish nothing if otherwise willing [readers, viewers and listeners] are not free to receive and consider them. It would be a barren marketplace of ideas that had only sellers and no buyers.").

† See West Virginia State Bd. of Educ. v. Barnette, 319 U.S. 624, 642 (1943) ("If there is any fixed star in our constitutional constellation, it is that no official, high or petty, can prescribe what shall be orthodox in politics, nationalism, religion, or other matters of opinion."); See also Ashcroft v. Free Speech Coalition, 535 U.S. 234, 245 (2002) ("[T]he First Amendment bars the government from dictating what we see or read or . . . hear.")

And so it is with "the freedom of speech." Our *individual* right to *receive* information and ideas is demonstrably broader than the rights of any speaker to *disseminate*. Each of us is entitled to receive information and ideas, even when there is no human "speaker" involved, and the government is prohibited from restricting that entitlement. This right encompasses our right to witness the wonders of nature in our everyday lives, to hear the wind rustling trees in the forest, to watch the sun rise or set, to gaze upon the stars above, to listen to the songs of birds, the bellowing calls of whales, the ocean's roar, the crack of lightning and thunder, and to observe all that is communicated to us through our senses—even when no human "speaker" generates anything recognizable as "speech." The same is true for information generated by machines—computers, and now, artificial intelligence.

Our freedom to receive, interpret, and make meaning of those words, images, symbols, and sounds is what the founders of our nation intended when they lumped the "freedom of speech" into the same constitutional provision as the freedom to decide which religious beliefs, if any, to embrace and espouse (speech, again), and to gather with others of like mind, in peaceable assembly.

Indeed, this conception of the First Amendment has been firmly embraced by the Supreme Court. That institution has repeatedly recognized that "the First Amendment goes beyond protection of the press and the self-expression of individuals to prohibit government from limiting the stock of information from which members of the public may draw."*

---

* *First National Bank of Boston v. Belloti*, 435 U.S. 765, 783(1978); *Va. Pharmacy Bd. v. Va. Consumer Council*, 425 U.S. 748 (1976) ("[Under the First Amendment's guarantee of the] Freedom of speech... the protection afforded is to the communication, to its source and to its recipients both"); *Red Lion Broadcasting Co. v. FCC*, 395 U.S. 367, 390 (1969) ("It is the right of the public to receive suitable access to social, political, esthetic,

That same court has also proclaimed, with crisp clarity, "the Constitution protects the right to receive information and ideas."[†]

Thus, both the founders of our nation and the justices of our highest court—two groups of leaders who are undeniably human and flawed, yet from whom we derive many of the basic legal and political understandings on which our democracy is based—have recognized and upheld the right to receive information alongside the right to disseminate it. It's an important concept. But it's one that can lead toward a second free speech metaphor that, like the first one, has significant flaws.

A major strand of First Amendment jurisprudence postulates a particular view of the right to receive information. This school of thought focuses less on the individual liberty conception of the right— freedom of thought—and more on the free flow of information as a necessary condition for collective self-governance. Premised on the eloquent words of James Madison, this strand of the right-to-receive-information doctrine proclaims that "A popular Government without popular information or the means of acquiring it, is but a Prologue to a Farce or a Tragedy, or perhaps both."

This instrumentalist view of the right posits that without access to accurate and truthful information, we the people cannot arrive at the "correct" answers to questions that confront us as a society. And there is undoubted truth to this: deprived of such information, our democracy would most surely perish. However, it can lead to an exceedingly narrow and even paternalistic definition of the information that the First Amendment prohibits the government from regulating,

---

moral, and other ideas and experiences which is crucial here."); *Martin v. City of Struthers*, 319 U.S. 141, 143 (1943) ("This freedom embraces the right to distribute literature . . . and necessarily protects the right to receive it.").

[†] *Kleindienst v. Mandel* , 408 U.S. 753, 763 (1972) (citations omitted).

restricting, or outright banning. For example, failed Supreme Court nominee Judge Robert Bork famously espoused the view that only information necessary to exercise the vote—"core political speech"—was within the freedom of speech. Therefore, in his view, government could act with impunity in limiting access to sculpture, paintings, comic books, and the like.

Unfortunately, this cramped view of the "right to receive information" has served, in large part, as the foundation for what has become the predominant metaphor for describing the freedom of speech—one that adopts a purely instrumentalist and collective notion of that right. A free flow of information is needed, this view postulates, exclusively to ensure that we, as a society, will discover and embrace "truth," reject false prophets and other charlatans, and collectively make "correct" choices.

The Freedom to Read Without Governmental Interference

While numerous judicial precedents have recognized that the First Amendment's guarantee of the freedom of speech protects our right to *receive information,* the landmark precedent that enshrined each individual's fundamental right to *read* whatever she chooses—even "obscene" material that, taken as whole, lacks serious literary, artistic, political, or scientific value—was the 1969 ruling in *Stanley v. Georgia.* In that case, an individual (one Robert E. Stanley) challenged his conviction for having violated a state statute that criminalized the knowing possession of obscene matter.* The Supreme Court ruled that the state statute could not be enforced because "the mere private possession of obscene matter cannot constitutionally be made a crime."†

---

* *Stanley v. Georgia,* 394 U.S. 557 (1969).

† *Id.* at 559.

Stanley is notable for several important propositions, not least of which is its explicit recognition that "[i]t is now well established that the First Amendment protects the right to receive information and ideas."‡ But even more important, it recognizes that the right to receive information *exceeds* even the rights of speakers, authors, and other information disseminators to distribute that information. The court acknowledged that the portion of Georgia's statute that criminalized the sale and distribution of obscene material—a narrowly cabined category of "unprotected speech"—was constitutional. After all, it held, society has a compelling interest in forestalling the distribution of information that appeals, in a "patently offensive manner," to one's "prurient interest" in nudity, sex, or excretion *and* that *also* lacks any serious literary, artistic, social or scientific value. The people, acting through their elected legislators, could exercise the collective police power of the state to keep such material out of the hands of impressionable members of society, including minors, by banning its distribution.

Nevertheless, a very different calculus applies when the government seeks to punish, through criminal penalties, those who merely *possess* (and presumably, therefore, wish to "consume" or view) such material. As the Court put it, "Th[e] right to receive information and ideas, *regardless of their social worth* . . . is fundamental to a free society."* The court recognized that "[t]he makers of our Constitution undertook to secure conditions favorable to the pursuit of happiness. . . . They sought *to protect Americans in their beliefs, their thoughts,* their emotions and their sensations."†

Acknowledging that Mr. Stanley challenged his conviction by asserting his "right to be free from state inquiry into the contents of his library," the court declared:

---

‡ *Id.* at 564 (citations omitted).
* *Id.* (emphasis added).
† *Id.* (citations omitted).

If the First Amendment means anything, it means a State has no business telling a man, sitting alone in his own house, what books he may read or what films he may watch. *Our whole national heritage rebels at the thought of giving government the power to control men's minds.*

... Whatever the power of the State to control the public dissemination of ideas inimical to morality, it cannot constitutionally premise legislation on the desirability of *controlling a person's private thoughts.*[*]

Stanley cited to, and quoted from, the most eloquent exposition of the individualistic, libertarian conception of the freedom of thought ever published in the pages of the *Supreme Court Reporter*—Justice Lewis Brandeis's concurrence in *Whitney v. California*:

[W]e must bear in mind why a State is, ordinarily, denied the power to prohibit dissemination of social, economic and political doctrine which a vast majority of its citizens believes to be false and fraught with evil consequence.

Those who won our independence believed that the final end of the State was to make men free to develop their faculties... They valued liberty both as an end, and as a means. ... They believed that freedom to think as you will and to speak

---

[*] *Id.* at 566 (italics added). The Supreme Court quoted from the dissenting opinion of Ohio Supreme Court Justice Thomas J. Herbert in *State v. Mapp,* 166 N.E. 2d 387, 393 (Ohio 1960) (J. Herbert, J., dissenting): "The right of an individual to read, to believe or disbelieve, and to think without governmental supervision is one of our basic liberties, but to dictate to the mature adult what books he may have in his private library seems ... to be a clear infringement of his constitutional rights as an individual."

as you think are means indispensable to the discovery and spread of political truth; that, without free speech and assembly, discussion would be futile; that, with them, discussion affords ordinarily adequate protection against the dissemination of noxious doctrine. . . .

Fear of serious injury cannot alone justify suppression of free speech and assembly. Men feared witches and burnt women. It is the function of speech to free men from the bondage of irrational fears. . . .

Those who won our independence by revolution were not cowards. They did not fear political change. They did not exalt order at the cost of liberty. To courageous, self-reliant men, with confidence in the power of free and fearless reasoning applied through the processes of popular government, *no danger flowing from speech can be deemed clear and present unless the incidence of the evil apprehended is so imminent that it may befall before there is opportunity for full discussion.* If there be time to expose through discussion the falsehood and fallacies, to avert the evil by the processes of education, the remedy to be applied is more speech, not enforced silence.*

In the decades following its landmark decision in *Stanley v. Georgia*, the Supreme Court, and lower courts across the land, recognized that the First Amendment not only prohibits government from *punishing* people for what they read, view, or think; it also bars government from monitoring those actions by acquiring, via search warrant or subpoena, library checkout or bookstore purchase records showing what

---

* *Whitney v. California*, 274 U.S. 357, 374-77 (1927) (Brandeis, J., concurring) (italics added).

individuals choose to read.* For example, in Colorado, Joyce Meskis, the late owner of the revered Tattered Cover bookstore in Denver, successfully challenged the efforts of a police department to obtain the purchase records of one of her store's customers, as part of a criminal investigation. Writing for the Colorado Supreme Court, Chief Justice Michael Bender said:

> Bookstores are places where a citizen can explore ideas, receive information, and discover myriad perspectives on every topic imaginable. When a person buys a book at a bookstore, he engages in activity protected by the First Amendment because he is exercising his right to read and receive ideas and information. Any *governmental* action that interferes with the willingness of customers to purchase books, or booksellers to sell books, thus implicates First Amendment concerns.
>
>   . . . [G]overnmental inquiry and intrusion into the reading choices of bookstore customers will almost certainly chill their constitutionally protected rights:
>
>   Once the government can demand of a publisher the names of the purchasers of his publications, the free press as we know it disappears. Then the spectre of a government agent will look over the shoulder of everyone who reads. . . . Fear of criticism goes with every person into the bookstall. The subtle,

---

* *See United States v. Rumely*, 345 U.S. 41, 57-58 (1953) (Douglas, J., concurring); *see also United States v. Playboy Entm't Group, Inc.*, 529 U.S. 803, 817 (2000) ("The citizen is entitled to seek out or reject certain ideas or influences without Government interference or control."); *In re Grand Jury Subpoena to Kramerbooks & Afterwords, Inc.*, 26 Media L. Rep. (BNA) 1599, 1601 (D.D.C. 1998) (requiring the government to "demonstrate a compelling interest in the information sought... [and] a sufficient connection between the [bookstore purchase records] and the grand jury investigation ....").

imponderable pressures of the orthodox lay hold. Some will fear to read what is unpopular, what the powers-that-be dislike. . . . Fear will take the place of freedom in the libraries, book stores, and homes of the land.

. . . In sum, the First Amendment embraces the individual's right to purchase and read whatever books she wishes to, without fear that the government will take steps to discover which books she buys, reads, or intends to read. A governmental search warrant directed to a bookstore that authorizes seizure of records that reflect a customer's purchases necessarily intrudes into areas protected by this right.*

From Marketplace to Endless Buffet

In what has become among the most quoted statements of any Supreme Court justice, Oliver Wendell Holmes, writing in dissent in 1919, declared that the First Amendment does not protect one who falsely shouts "fire" in a crowded theater and thereby triggers an instantaneous, unthinking, reflexive response causing physical injury. In so pronouncing, Holmes offered a metaphor for the freedom of speech that has endured in Supreme Court lore and jurisprudence ever after. He espoused the view that "*the ultimate good* desired is better reached by *free trade* in ideas—that the best test of truth is the power of the thought to get itself accepted in *the competition of the market* . . . . That, at any rate, is the theory of our Constitution.'"*

---

* *Tattered Cover v. City of Thornton*, 44 P.3d 1044, 1052-53 (Colo. 2002).

* *Abrams v. United States*, 250 U.S. 616, 630 (1919) (Holmes, J., dissenting) (italics added).

The Supreme Court repeated this same view as recently as 2012: "The remedy for speech that is false is speech that is true. This is the ordinary course in a free society. The response to the unreasoned is the rational; to the uninformed, the enlightened; to the straight-out lie, the simple truth."[†] At its heart, Holmes' "marketplace of ideas" metaphor posits an open, unregulated "free exchange" of views, in which all speakers may hold forth, be heard by all, and effectively counter "false" and "bad" doctrine with "true" and "good" doctrine. In this instrumentalist view, the latter set of views will inevitably prevail over the former ones and be adopted by the consumers of the competing statements.

But as others have pointed out, the "marketplace of ideas" is an inappropriate metaphor to capture what the First Amendment protects.[‡] Unregulated markets of goods and services produce profits for some purveyors while driving others out of business. By no means do the producers and distributors of "better" products always win out over inferior ones; see, for example, the competition between VHS and Betamax home video formats. More important, marketplaces do not produce, and are not expected to produce, truth. Nor does a "free competition among ideas or theories" in open debates or public forums. necessarily produce a triumph for truth; witness social media, and those who violently stormed the Capitol on January 6, 2021, many of whom firmly believed they were "taking our country back from the

---

[†] *United States v. Alvarez*, 567 U.S. 709, 728 (2012) (quoting *Abrams v. United States*, 250 U.S. 616, 630 (1919) (Holmes, J., dissenting)).

[‡] *See, e.g.*, John G. Francis and Leslie P. Francis, *Freedom of Thought in the United States: The First Amendment, Marketplaces of Ideas, and the Internet* (U. of Utah 2021), https://dc.law.utah.edu/cgi/view-content.cgi?article=1302&context=scholarship; Morgan Weiland, *First Amendment Metaphors: The Death of the 'Marketplace of Ideas' and the Rise of the Post-Truth 'Free Flow of Information,'* 33:3 Yale J. of L. and the Hum. 366 (2022).

traitors." So the notion that a "free exchange of ideas" will inevitably result in the emergence of "truth" is empirically and historically incorrect.

More fundamentally, however, the free interchange of ideas does not need to produce "correct" answers or "truth" to be worthwhile and protected from government intrusion. It is the freedom to decide which ideas we each choose to subscribe to—*right or wrong*—that constitutes the freedom of speech. Each of us can be held accountable by our society for the *actions* we take, whether motivated by those thoughts and beliefs or not.* But we cannot be held accountable for what we believe or think.

The rights protected by the First Amendment are not strictly limited to speech, religion, or association with those of similar beliefs— they encompass all the freedoms included in the freedom of thought. And to decide which ideas and beliefs each of chooses to subscribe to, we need, and we are guaranteed by the First Amendment, to receive a full, unfiltered, unregulated stream of ideas and information. Not a marketplace where the best idea or truth will inevitably carry the day, but a bookstore or library, where we each can decide for ourselves what information, *correct or not*, we wish to consider. The government can regulate our actions, but not our thoughts, and it cannot limit the stock of information we draw upon to form those thoughts. Today, the physical space of a bookstore or library has been expanded, virtually, through the internet, courtesy of Amazon and myriad other booksellers, online libraries, and a seemingly infinite, ever-growing number of information providers. All may be accessed freely thanks to the First Amendment.

---

* "Among free men, the deterrents ordinarily to be applied to prevent crime are education and punishment for violations of the law. . . ." *Whitney v. California*, 274 U.S. 357, 379 (1927) (Brandeis, J., concurring).

While the Supreme Court has rejected the proposition that the Constitution requires the government to provide information to the public, several of our nation's founders recognized that public education and public libraries were essential means of ensuring a well-informed and functioning democracy. Whether access to books, movies, audio recordings, and other sources of information is provided by public funds or private sources, the bookstore and library provide a far more robust embodiment of what the freedom of speech encompasses than does the metaphor of "the marketplace of ideas." The literary offerings of such repositories, not limited to political speech but embracing every form of creative expression—however fantastical, imaginary, and even the undeniably false (i.e., the Earth is flat)—is the far more appropriate metaphor for what it means to live a free society, one in which government is strictly forbidden from punishing or restricting the *thoughts* of individuals.

Only harmful, or potentially harmful, *actions* may be subject to governmental regulation; under the First Amendment, there is simply no such thing as a punishable or unlawful thought.* And the metaphorical symbol of countless shelves of books and other content, extending indefinitely into space through ever-evolving technologies, aptly signifies that intellectual freedom: an infinite buffet of ideas and information upon which each of us is at liberty to feast.

---

* Of course, certain crimes, like extortion, fraud, or conspiracy, can be committed through spoken words alone.

14.
The First Amendment: Standing Our Ground with Joyce

Betsy Burton

Betsy Burton co-founded The King's English Bookshop in 1977 and co-owned it until 2021 when she retired and sold her majority interest to longtime California book professional Calvin Crosby. Burton served on local and regional bookseller boards over the years; she was an ABA Board member from 2009 to 2015 and ABA Board president from 2016 to 2017. She wrote and published a book, The King's English: Adventures of an Independent Bookseller, *in 2005; produced an independent documentary on the police and the special-needs population entitled* Invisible Disabilities *in 2012; published, edited, and still writes for the* Inkslinger, *her store's book magazine; and has also reviewed books on KUER, the local NPR station, for many years. She still shops avidly at The King's English and is currently working her way through long Covid by writing a book about her special-needs son with her husband, Kit Burton.*

T ORN DOESN'T BEGIN TO DESCRIBE my state of mind as I sit at my desk weighing the longtime love, respect, and gratitude I feel for Joyce Meskis against my misgivings about trying to craft a chapter for a book about her.

Joyce and I opened our bookstores at about the same time (the Tattered Cover in 1974, The King's English in 1977). We were members and officers of the same regional and national bookseller organizations. We traded everything from war stories to best practices for years. I owe her so much. We all do.

Yet my eighteen-month-long (and ongoing) bout with long Covid and the challenges our family faces due to my son's struggles with his health seem to make the attempt to marshal my distant memories of Joyce almost overwhelming.

But as I mull those memories, flooded by the reality of all that *we do* owe Joyce Meskis, I'm struck by one thing that I hadn't considered before. On top of the unending gratitude booksellers all acknowledge owing her for her work on behalf of free speech, for the essential bulwark she erected for us thanks to her unending, eloquent insistence on the vital nature of the First Amendment, and her fierce and seemingly endless fight to shore up our defense of free expression in the face of every challenge from local school boards to the federal government (remember the so-called Patriot Act?)—on top of all that, I owe her gratitude for something *beyond* that bulwark: the freedom I subsequently felt, we have all felt, to pursue other things we believed would enable our survival as booksellers.

In my case, it was the Local First movement, which I believed and still believe is vital to our fight against Amazon and the chains. When Joyce and I opened the Tattered Cover and The King's English respectively, bookselling was easy: Local stores each had their own niche, the only chains were B. Dalton and Walden's, and making payroll just wasn't that hard. Then the big chains came to town—stores that carried everything, discounted everything, and got preferential treatment from the government, the public, and publishers alike (which, of course, made it possible for them to discount everything)—and suddenly life became much more difficult for all of us.

We indies responded by educating independent publishers about strategies that could make us competitive against the chains—and by educating the public about the importance of independent bookstores. ABA initiatives, from Local First to Indies First and Indie Next to Indies Introduce, emphasized not only the importance of local business to our economy and our communities but also the vital nature of independent bookstores to the book industry as a whole.

I'm happy to say these strategies have worked—which is why our survival has turned into our revival. Our indie renaissance.

But none of this would have been possible without Joyce Meskis. Simply put, had Joyce not so thoroughly vanquished foes of the First Amendment for so many years, none of us would have been free to pursue these other issues essential for our self-preservation as booksellers. The First Amendment in general and freedom of expression in particular, whether in public forums or in print, are basic principles without which none among us could exist. Or at least not for long.

I realize something else as I sit here remembering her. I believe that Joyce Meskis would be fighting still, like the tigress she was, had she witnessed what I consider the fall from grace of the American Booksellers Association. I'm referring to the changes made in the ABA Ends Policies by the ABA board in September 2021—changes that I and many of my fellow booksellers view as an abandonment of the principle of free expression.

At the time, I argued vehemently against those changes. I understand the anger felt by some board members (and some of my fellow booksellers) at the protection the First Amendment can afford to those who say harmful things, give pain, and wreak havoc in the world. But I simply cannot understand their refusal to acknowledge that, without that First Amendment protection, we are all lost.

Here is my attempt to argue that point. I wrote it pre-Covid and therefore, I hope, more articulately than what I have written above. It's my attempt to advocate for what Joyce Meskis held most dear and to offer a further bulwark against its loss.

Dear Booksellers,

Margaret Atwood said in a 2022 interview with Carolyn Kellogg in the *L.A Times*, "People are deeply worried about the future right now . . . partly because democratic norms and procedures that we took for granted and believed represented the true, the good and the beautiful, have been tossed out the window."[*] That sentence seems to capture exactly my ongoing feelings of betrayal and sadness in reaction to the ABA's removal of the ideal of freedom of expression from our Ends Policies—that they had tossed my most cherished ideal right out the window—a tenet that has seen me through a lifetime of bookselling, standing me in good stead whenever books were censored, edited, or outright banned, giving me the tools (both legal and moral) to defend books against such attacks.

Isn't the highest and best calling of booksellers and librarians to put books in the hands of readers? Surely not to pick and choose among the books readers should or should not read. Am I wrong?

---

[*] Carolyn Kellogg, "Margaret Atwood is not your 'elderly icon' or 'witchy granny.' She's better than that," *Los Angeles Times,* February 24, 2022, https://www.latimes.com/entertainment-arts/books/story/2022-02-24/margaret-atwood-is-not-your-elderly-icon-or-witchy-granny-shes-better-than-that#:~:text=Audiences%20want%20to%20hear%20from,-from%20her%20home%20in%20Canada.

Herein lies the question. Do we have the right to choose which books to protect and which to throw out the window? The ABA Board would argue that we do. According to them, "ABA does not favor the protection of free expression when it comes to speech that violates our commitment to equity and antiracism, i.e., racist speech, anti-Semitic speech, homophobic speech, transphobic speech, etc." In their 2022 FAQ on the subject, they explain their need to be in a position to *condemn* such books (italics mine).

Which raises further questions: Who decides which books to protect and which books not to? What standards do they employ to decide? What does the ABA intend to do with books that they have deemed unfit?

a. Ban them?

b. Burn them?

This might seem an Orwellian sort of *reductio ad absurdum*. And in one way it is. Because there *is* no rational answer, at least if one believes in the First Amendment. Either protect all books or throw the First Amendment out the window. Any halfway measure leads to a world without First Amendment protections—a dangerous world indeed, as such events as the Salem witch trials and Nazi book burnings (to name just two among many terrifying events throughout the history) exemplify.

As Atwood so succinctly responded, when asked, in the above-mentioned article, about the Martin Luther King, Jr., quote stating that the arc of history bends toward justice, "Love it. It's just not true."

In summation, we urgently need answers from the ABA board to three questions:

1. If we as an association defend banning books, on what possible grounds do we object to others banning books they don't approve of?

2. If you *do* intend to uphold the protection of free expression as the ABA has done historically, why not reinstate it as an Ends Policy?

3. If you *do not* intend such protection to be universal, *what* exactly do you plan to do with those books you deem unworthy? *Who* decides? Based on *what* criteria?

Without First Amendment protection—nationwide and within the book industry—it is not the dogs of war that will be unleashed, but rather the dogs of suppression. Sadly, we will be the first victims.

Betsy Burton

I would never have summoned up the moxie to write such a letter had I not been inspired--early on and for my entire professional life—by the passionate spirit and principled beliefs of Joyce Meskis. I miss her in more ways than I can say.

15.
Freedom of Expression— Messy, Contentious, Painful, and Essential: One Publisher's Perspective

Karl Weber

For a brief description of Karl Weber's work and career, see "About the Editor" on page 239.

I 'VE BEEN PRACTICING freedom of expression, and occasionally paying the price for it, since at least 1969. That was the year when, as my punishment for serving as the 16-year-old editor and publisher of a so-called underground newspaper named *The Rajpramukh Ball-ute,* I was relieved of my full scholarship to the private Rhodes School in Manhattan and exiled for twelfth grade to Ft. Hamilton High School, the public school closest to my home in Bay Ridge, Brooklyn.

My mom was hopping mad—at her wayward, rebellious son, not at the school administrators who punished me for exercising my freedom of speech. But in a funny way, it all worked out perfectly for me. If

I hadn't been in Mr. Pelkonen's senior English class at Ft. Hamilton, I might never have met a girl with purple-dyed hair to whom I've now been happily married for fifty years.

So, yeah, the spirit of free expression and I go way back. And in times like the present, when the freedom to say, write, read, and publish whatever we like is once again under assault, I'm happy to join other book lovers in reaffirming my allegiance to that spirit.

Given the rising tide of censorship in today's America, I'm grateful to the attorneys, booksellers, librarians, and civil rights activists who have devoted their lives to speaking out on behalf of freedom of expression and defending it through practical, hands-on actions: making powerful arguments in court, selling books the would-be censors would squelch, and giving young people access to ideas and information no matter where they may live. They remind us why the freedom to speak, read, and write is so fundamental to our democracy. (There's a good reason why the founders put that freedom in the *First* Amendment, the bedrock on which all our other liberties rests.)

But sometimes I think we get a little tangled up and confused in the way we talk about free expression. I've been struggling to sort out the issues for myself. Let me share what I've come up with so far.

I'll start with the bedrock—the First Amendment. People often speak as if the First Amendment says all there is to say about freedom of speech. Yes, it's fundamental. But it doesn't have *all* the answers.

Remember that the First Amendment—like the rest of the U.S. Constitution—is about how our government should work. It asserts the principle that government mustn't get into the business of censoring the press—period. We all know there have been times and places where uniformed thugs have smashed printing presses and where journalists, scholars, novelists, and poets have been jailed for producing work that those in government hated. The First Amendment declares, "Not in America."

There's more. Thanks to the First Amendment, when government actions impact the dissemination of published works—for example, when public libraries and schools make choices about the books they'll buy and circulate—the values guiding those actions must be ideologically and political neutral, or at least as close to neutrality as is humanly possible.

These principles embedded in the First Amendment establish a wall against governmental censorship that is a crucial bastion of American liberty.

But the First Amendment doesn't govern the actions of private actors. Governments can't stop writers, editors, and publishers from producing any content they want. Writers, editors, and publishers are and must be free to make their own judgments about the content they want to publish. And those who read and use books and other writings—individual readers, booksellers, librarians, schoolteachers, and many others—have the same freedom to choose what they will use *and what they will reject.*

And here, I think, is where conversations about free speech start to get messy.

The judgments we make about writing, reading, publishing, and distributing particular books are inevitably fraught; they are never "value-free." This poses real challenges for all of us in the world of books—editors, publishers, booksellers, librarians, and all the other members of what we might call "the publishing chain." That's especially true in times like today, when culture, information, ideas, and even personal identities have become, like so much else, intensely politicized. Controversies now routinely explode not just about books that are overtly political (tracts and manifestos) but about novels, plays, memoirs, textbooks, even children's picture books. It sometimes seems as though every decision we make about publishing a book or supporting an author—or refusing to do so—subjects us to criticism or attack by someone who claims to be offended or assaulted by our choice.

Let's face it: In the world of 2024, publishing is a political act.

For some of us, that's neither a surprise nor a problem. There have always been writers, editors, publishers, booksellers, and librarians who view their work as an act of political engagement. Some approach it from a liberal ("left") perspective, others from a conservative ("right") one. Either way, such politically engaged book people are comfortable thinking about the political impact of the books they produce—and many of them are accustomed to defending their ideas in the public square. That's politics, after all.

But lots of book people do *not* think of themselves as doing political work. Many—perhaps most—fell in love with books for reasons that are deeply personal, emotional, and aesthetic.

Personal disclosure: As it happens, I've lived my life in both of these publishing camps. Yes, when I was 16, I was an "underground publisher" courting trouble with the school authorities for my supposedly "radical" views on issues like the Vietnam War. But at the time, I thought of myself mainly as a poet, and I spent the next several years of my life as an English major, eventually earning a master's degree for my dissertation on the religious poetry of Emily Dickinson. So, yes, I understand how publishing is a political act . . . but I also understand the urge to scrawl lines of verse in little booklets to be stored in a secret drawer for no one in the world to see.

Moved by our aesthetic passions, many of us in publishing think of literature as something above—or at least clearly separate from—the often distasteful, sometimes dishonest, and occasionally violent world of politics. And so we're appalled to find ourselves, our decisions, and the books we publish being judged and sometimes attacked on political grounds.

It feels terrible when that happens. And in our search for ways to escape the discomfort, it's easy to fall back on the First Amendment as offering a seemingly simple solution. "How dare you criticize me for publishing that book?" we declare. "Haven't you ever heard of *the First Amendment!?*"

The problem is that, when we lean on the First Amendment in this way, we sometimes end up lumping together issues and problems that are not identical. In particular, we may fall into the trap of speaking as if the First Amendment should protect us from *private* attacks on our freedom to publish. The First Amendment erects a wall against government censorship; it doesn't say anything about the behavior of private individuals. And as we know, there are times when private individuals hate particular ideas so deeply that they desperately want to discourage the publication and spread of books that promote those ideas.

If you think the sentence you just read couldn't possibly refer to anyone you know, you might think again. You may be ready to defend to the death the right of everyone from public library patrons to middle school students to read such often-banned books as *The Bluest Eye, The Handmaid's Tale,* and *The 1619 Project.* Good for you! But would you feel exactly the same about *Mein Kampf, The Protocols of the Elders of Zion,* and *The Turner Diaries*? Would you be outraged by a bookseller who refuses to stock one of the books in that second group? Maybe you would—but I don't think the "right" answers to these questions are necessarily obvious.

My point is that, while the First Amendment protects all these works against government censorship, it doesn't stop private people from rejecting them—nor should it.

SOME SAY, "Isn't it just as bad to have private people trying to silence you as when the government does it? Does it really make a difference who the would-be censors are?"

My response is, Yeah, it *does* make a difference—a big one. Here are three reasons why I think so.

First, the government acts on behalf of all of us, in the name of the people (or the nation, or the state) and uses resources provided by all of us when we pay our taxes. For the government to single out specific voices and perspectives to be squelched when it purports to represent and defend the interests of all is unfair and tyrannical. When it comes to beliefs and attitudes on which citizens differ, the government must be neutral—not laying its heavy thumb on the scales for partisan or sectarian reasons.

Second, the government is made up of individuals who wield power delegated to them by all of us. Those individuals have a vested interest in hanging on to that power—which is why it's so important that their access to that power should be strictly defined, limited, and subject to revocation by the people. (The resulting conflicts are another part of what we refer to as politics.) Letting politicians control the public expression of ideas inevitably tempts them to use that control to hang on to or expand their power—to turn public channels of expression into vehicles for propaganda. That's why politicians are the very last people we should trust with decisions about what should and should not be published.

Third, the reach of government is deep and powerful, and becoming more so. When one or two bureaucrats in a small agency try to censor an idea, that's bad, but the harm is usually limited. But when those at the top of government make a concerted effort to promote some ideas and to stifle others, the impact can be huge. We can see this at work today in a state like Florida, where a governor wedded to a particular ideology has been using his power to push conformity to that ideology through a range of tools: high school curricula, state college governance, public library regulations, and punitive financial and legal assaults on offending private corporations.

So when governments seek to censor, it's outrageously unfair, it undermines democracy, and it's potentially very destructive. By contrast, when private individuals take offense at particular ideas and their expression, they speak for no one but themselves; they do not wield public money or power; and they have little practical ability to punish or harm those who disagree. Private would-be censors may be (and often are) foolish, annoying, and uncivil. But the damage they can do is minimal compared to what public censors can do.

We've all seen pictures of bonfires in which books and works of art are being consumed. They're archetypal images of the evils of censorship. But history shows that it matters who's doing the burning. When Nazis allied with Germany's fascist government burned books by Jewish authors in 1933, it was a step toward a Holocaust that murdered millions. When DJs in the American South burned Beatles albums in 1966, it was a silly stunt that exposed their own impotence—and did practically nothing to limit the cultural impact of the Beatles.

My point? I'm no fan of the spirit of censorship. And I am *not* excusing or endorsing book burning—by anyone! But not all acts of censorship are the same. And not all criticisms leveled at ideas—or at their expression in books—is censorship. These distinctions are real, and they matter.

So far, I've been speaking about these issues in abstract terms. Maybe a couple of concrete examples will clarify what I'm saying.

Consider, for example, the events surrounding Jeanne Cummins's novel *American Dirt*. You likely know the outlines of the story: The book, which tells a story of violence and fear set on the southern border of the U.S., was published in January 2020 by Flatiron Books, a division of the Big-Five publishing house Macmillan. It arrived on a wave of favorable publicity and bookseller enthusiasm, beginning long before publication, when the draft manuscript attracted interest from a host of editors and earned its author a career-changing seven-figure advance. Oprah selected *American Dirt* for her television book club, further anointing the title as a likely bestseller.

Then the backlash began. It started with a blog post by a California-based writer named Myriam Gurba, who'd been asked to review *American Dirt* by *Ms.* Magazine. Her review was so scathing that *Ms.* refused to publish it, so it ended up on Gurba's blog instead. Gurba hated everything about the book. She considered its characters and story sterotyped, false, and condescending—a mere caricature of the Latino people for whom it purported to speak. She also hated the way the publisher was promoting the book, starting with the phrase "these people" used in a publicist's cover letter to refer to Latino people. Gurba's anger was red-hot on the page.

A furor erupted. Some voices from the Latino world sided with Gurba; others did not. Some people who had long bemoaned the failure of mainstream book publishing to amplify the voices of minority communities (Latin, Black, Asian, LGBTXQ+, and so on) seized on *American Dirt* as an example. There was talk of picket lines and demonstrations, and even a couple of bomb threats aimed at booksellers. The jittery publisher canceled part of the extensive book tour it had planned for Cummins.

Here I must make one very important point, which perhaps should be obvious but which needs to be made explicit: *Any act of violence, real or threatened, is inexcusable—not a form of "speech" deserving of legal or social protection.* I think harsh criticism of ideas is fine; I think the same about peaceful demonstrations and boycotts, under most circumstances. But violence, even when deployed on behalf of ideological goals, is very different. It's not about expressing an opinion; it's about using power to impose your will on another person, and that is never permissible in a free society.

This distinction between free speech and threats of violence is clearly recognized by the law. The First Amendment doesn't protect people who use speech to foment riots or instigate attacks. I think we all need to recognize that distinction, too.

Unfortunately, many of the people who hear about cases like the saga of *American Dirt*, lump all the attacks on the book—the blog posts, the angry articles, the demonstrations, the boycotts, and the death threats—into a single undifferentiated mass described as "censorship" or "cancellation." As a result, the story is widely viewed as an example of how freedom of expression is under siege in the U.S. Not only do many people believe that Jeanne Cummins was the victim of a vicious mob-like assault; many also claim that the episode represents the triumph of a new regime in which book publishers operate in terror, unable or unwilling to publish anything that might run afoul of critics like Myriam Gurba.

Thus, in January 2023, *New York Times* columnist Pamela Paul (formerly editor of the *Times Book Review*), wrote a column revisiting the story, in which she said:

> Looking back now, it's clear that the "American Dirt" debacle of January 2020 was a harbinger, the moment when the publishing world lost its confidence and ceded moral authority to the worst impulses of its detractors. . . . Books that would once have been greenlit are now passed over; sensitivity readers are employed on a regular basis; self-censorship is rampant.
>
> A creative industry that used to thrive on risk-taking now shies away from it. And it all stemmed from a single writer posting a discursive and furious takedown of "American Dirt" and its author on a minor blog.

Paul's column drew 1,168 published reader comments, the overwhelming majority of which endorsed Paul's analysis of the story and decried the apparent power of critics like Gurba to destroy worthy books and the lives of their authors.

I think this reaction is a serious misreading of what really happened. For all the talk of "censorship" and "silencing," the novel was *not* removed from bookstore or libraries, but in fact became a massive bestseller, earning a huge amount of money for the author, her publisher, and others in the publishing chain. Cummins appeared on the *Oprah* show to discuss the book as planned—alongside a couple of critics invited to offer their own perspectives on the book. And to this day, her publisher continues to distribute *American Dirt* and has publicly declared it fully intends to publish her future work when it's ready.

Yes, Cummins was subject to criticism, some of it personal and harsh. Welcome to the world of social media. I'm sure she hated being on the receiving end of these attacks—God knows I would. But she and her book also received plenty of positive attention, including both laudatory reviews and, most concretely, enormous sales and income. Neither her career nor her life has been "destroyed." And I don't see the U.S. publishing scene as being controlled by terror of some "woke mob" enforcing ideological conformity.

(In her column, Pamela Paul claimed that Cummins has "become something of a pariah among her professional peers," and then cited as evidence that fact that "Since publication, I have been told, not a single author in America has asked her to blurb a book." I'm not sure whether that should be considered a loss or a relief.)

Add it all up, and, if this is what it's like to be "cancelled," I think there are plenty of other novelists who would welcome such cancellation.

LET'S TAKE A STEP BACK to consider what the story of *American Dirt* really tells us.

The arguments raised on both sides about the book and its reception are important and worthy of discussion. They have obvious political implications: those criticizing *American Dirt* mainly do so from a perspective that might broadly be characterized as liberal, left-wing, or progressive; some (not all) of those defending it have done so, in part, because they disagree with a range of left-wing cultural and political attitudes. Against this backdrop, smart, thoughtful people who care about literature and American culture have reached varying conclusions about the merits of the novel. People also disagree about the content and tone of the criticisms leveled against *American Dirt,* sometimes influenced by whose-ox-is-gored considerations. (As a dyed-in-the-wool liberal, my instinctive reaction is to want to defend things my fellow liberals say. If I were a conservative, my instincts would probably run in the opposite direction. Over the decades, I've learned that it's important for me *not* to automatically indulge my instincts, because they can be misleading. But they still affect my emotions, as I suspect is true for most people.)

All of these reactions, and the debates they stimulate, are natural and appropriate.

What's *not* helpful is the cacophony of voices citing the First Amendment to say, in effect, that the harsh criticism *American Dirt* received from some people represented an illegitimate and dangerous threat to free expression.

Here's an example of what I mean, from a 2020 column by film and book critic Neal Pollack. He uses the *American Dirt* controversy as an example of what he calls "the new censorship":

The "censorial spirit" is baked into the American DNA. No one makes small-town idiots quite as idiotic as we do. But our robust First Amendment and the greatest publishing industry in the history of the world has always beaten back that spirit. Of all the American virtues, freedom of expression is number one. . . . So I find it depressing that the censorial spirit has risen in a new form. But this time, the censorship is coming from inside the house.

When Pollack says that the new censorship "is coming from inside the house," he means that people *within* the publishing world—writers, critics, staffers at publishing companies—are criticizing and sometimes even protesting specific books. Pollack lists a series of cases that he describes as examples of this "recent, and dangerous trend," calling them "hallmarks of the new censorship." His examples include memoirs by film maker Woody Allen and political controversialist Milo Yiannopoulos, both of which had contracts cancelled by their publishers. Then he turns to Cummins's novel:

> The new censorial era entered a heightened phase earlier this year with the eruption of the *American Dirt* controversy. Author Jeanne Cummins, a white woman, dared to write a novel about immigration. More significantly, she received a seven-figure advance and an Oprah's Book Club selection. Another author derided *American Dirt* as "pity porn." Later, nearly 100 prominent authors signed a letter that read, in part, "But good intentions do not make good literature, particularly not when the execution is so faulty, and the outcome so harmful." Flatiron Books, having invested way too much money into *American Dirt*'s success, kept it on the shelves, but canceled Cummins' book tour out of fear for her safety.

I don't mean to single out Pollack particularly. His arguments have been echoed by countless commentators in recent years. You may find yourself nodding as you read them. But here's why I think they're flawed, just as Pamela Paul's column was flawed.

We're all free to form our own opinions about each of these controversies. If you were a publisher charged with making a decision about publishing any one of these books, you might respond in a number of ways based on various factors. The same goes for booksellers and librarians after a book is published. But I find it unhelpful to simply lump all of these stories of books facing public pushback together under the same heading of "the new censorship" and to claim or imply that the First Amendment renders all these controversies equivalent—and the criticisms leveled inappropriate and indefensible.

When we make that sort of blanket statement, we obscure the specific on-the-ground realities that makes these cases much more complicated than one might like. What's more, phrases like "the new censorship" and some of the other charged language often used around stories like these—"cancel culture," "mob rule," "PC thought police," "vigilantism," "silencing speech," and the like—tend to make those who criticize books appear far more powerful, ruthless, and dangerous than they really are.

Many of the other cases cited by polemicists like Pollack resemble that of *American Dirt* in that the books did *not* end up being "cancelled," "silenced," or otherwise "censored." The contract to publish Woody Allen's memoir, for example, was cancelled by one publisher after junior staffers protested. But the book was then published by another house, Skyhorse Publishing, run by a self-proclaimed maverick who prides himself on his willingness to publish books outside the mainstream culture and has built a very successful business doing so. More power to him!

Similarly, Milo Yiannopoulos chose to self-publish the memoir that Simon & Schuster cancelled; it appeared on a host of bestseller lists, including those of the *New York Times,* the *Wall Street Journal,* and *USA Today.* His political influence has since faded, due not to left-wing "censorship" but due to distracting controversies over issues like sexual consent, which led to his having a speaking invitation cancelled by the Conservative Political Action Conference—not exactly a bastion of the "woke mob."

These stories illustrate how the free market and the First Amendment are supposed to work—and do. Neither has been weakened, much less destroyed, by the likes of Myriam Gurba or those who criticized Woody Allen and Milo Yiannopoulos.

SOME PEOPLE SEEM TO THINK—perhaps they would like to believe—that publishing decisions can somehow be made non-controversial, as if removed entirely from the sphere of politics. For example, I've heard colleagues in publishing say that we members of the publishing chain should simply reflect and respond to public demand when making business decisions: "Let's publish every imaginable kind of book, and leave it up to readers to decide what they want." This makes it sound as though content decisions can be separated from moral, cultural, intellectual, and political values and treated simply as neutral responses to economic realities.

If this were true, then content decisions would be mere applications of objective facts: "Is there sufficient demand for this content to make it profitable? If so, then we should publish it. If not, then we should not." Values wouldn't come into the question—which would mean there is never any ground to criticize the participants in the publishing chain, who are simply responding to objective market pressures in a purely neutral, value-free way.

But this is not an accurate reflection of how the book business works, for several reasons.

First, everyone in the publishing chain has made basic prior choices about the kinds of content they will focus on, in terms of category, genre, market, format, sales channels, author background, and more. These choices inevitably reflect personal or organizational interests, preferences, and goals—in short, values.

Second, our knowledge of "what readers want" is incomplete and inaccurate, which is why there are so many books that fail in the market (as well as many unexpected successes). The reality is that most publishing decisions are crapshoots facing varying odds of success, chosen not only for value-free economic reasons but also because of hunches, instincts, impulses, "love," and other emotional reactions on the part of publishers. These emotional reactions are also heavily influenced by our values.

Most important, publishers do not merely passively respond to a reader marketplace that is autonomous and independent. They help to shape that marketplace by the publishing choices they make. Whenever a publisher brings a new book to the marketplace—especially one that is original and unusual in any way—they are making a deliberate effort to affect reader preferences by stimulating curiosity, interest, and demand. These efforts sometimes succeed and sometimes fail. But in every case, they reflect publisher choices about what to publish and how to promote it—which, again, are unavoidably value-laden.

There's a second, more subtle way in which we sometimes misunderstand the publishing process. I've heard publishing professionals—smart, talented people whose work I admire—acknowledge that publishing decisions are, inevitably, based on subjective judgments, but then fall back on the claim that these judgments are simply based on objective standards of "quality." They say things like, "Well, of course, we exercise our editorial judgment when we choose the books we publish. But we're not supposed to choose books because we like their message or because we agree with the author's views. We will publish any book that is well written and important. Otherwise, we would become nothing more than mouthpieces for some chosen ideology, and the books we publish would be nothing but propaganda."

This sounds sensible and even wise—but I think its underlying logic is a little squishy. Terms like "well-written," "important," "serious," "worthy of publication," "a contribution to the national debate," and so on, inevitably "smuggle in" value judgments. (One of the best editors I know once made the case to me that his editorial choices were basically value-free and driven simply by "editorial quality." But then, unprompted, he went on to add, "Of course, I doubt I would ever publish a book by that crackpot Jordan Peterson." Maybe the difference between us is purely semantic . . . but I think my editor friend's "values" were peeking through in that statement. Not that there's anything wrong with that!)

In the end, I think both of these flawed analyses are based on an underlying fallacy—the belief that publishers have an obligation to be "neutral" when it comes to their values.

First of all, as I've suggested, that's not even possible. In the end, we have no choice but to make the hard decisions. We have to decide what values we want to espouse and support. And that's okay! Acknowledging the role that values play in publishing decisions does *not* mean reducing publishing to "propaganda," nor does it mean that publishers should only publish books they agree with. It does mean that values are inevitably part of the decision-making process, and they deserve to be discussed openly when those decisions are being made.

I'm not arguing that an editor or publisher should only support books or authors whose ideas they share and support. That would make publishing a boring job! And in practice, it would be almost impossible, since very few people agree about *everything*. (Ask anyone who has been married about that.) In reality, publishers publish books that fall along a continuum from those with which they fervently agree to those that contain ideas and value judgments they find dubious or even just plain wrong.

That, too, is natural and even desirable. In fact, it can be especially valuable for a publisher to publish a book by an author whose values they are somewhat uneasy with! Bring those questions to the editorial process. Challenge the author to address your doubts and to defend his arguments. (I've done this with authors countless times, as have most good editors.) The result is often a better book—one that might even stand a chance of bridging some of the partisan divides in our society.

So I'm not advocating for an editorial process that is driven by a set of rigid moral or political benchmarks. But I am saying that it's perfectly legitimate for a publisher to refuse to publish a particular book because they believe it espouses values that are repugnant or harmful to society. Importantly, it's also perfectly legitimate for a different publisher to make the opposite decision about the same book, and they *must* be free to do so.

And the fact that these decisions are fraught and not black and white also means that we should expect to have them questioned, challenged, even denounced. That's okay, too. (That's why they pay us publishing executives the big bucks—or least the big-ish bucks.)

For this reason, it's legitimate for individuals—inside or outside publishers—to express their opinions about the values espoused by a book, and even to do so in ways that might be obtrusive and vociferous—so long as they don't employ violence or obstruct the rights of others to express their own opinions and act accordingly. So when the young employees of a publishing company sign a petition criticizing the company management for publishing a book they consider politically repugnant or dangerous, they are perfectly within their rights. And the company management is free to react according to their best judgment, depending on many, many factors (including the possible impact on company morale, the expected profitability of the proposed book, its literary and other merits, and—yes—the political values of the company leaders themselves).

In a case like this, no one on either side is guilty of violating anyone's First Amendment rights—though there will probably be op-ed articles and letters to newspaper editors that accuse them of doing so.

Let's return one last time to the example of *American Dirt.* I think American Booksellers for Free Expression—the arm of the American Booksellers Association dedicated to freedom of expression—got it right when they addressed the controversy. Here's an excerpt from the statement they issued on February 5, 2020:

ABFE believes that the conversations about *American Dirt* are not only protected by the First Amendment, but that they are essential in a society founded on democratic ideals. It is crucial that all voices are heard.

The fullest expression of the First Amendment is that it protects the voices of the oppressed, the underrepresented, and the marginalized. Unfortunately, history has shown all too often that these are the voices silenced by a government's failure to respect the right of free expression for all.

ABFE supports the challenging, and sometimes difficult, conversations and dialogue surrounding *American Dirt*. Importantly, ABFE strongly supports the rights of bookstores to stock—or not to stock—American Dirt, and, also, to host the author, if they choose. ABFE also strongly supports the rights of those opposed to, or offended by, the book to protest.

ABFE strongly opposes attempts to block the sale of any book as well as any actions expressly intended to cancel author or book events regarding *American Dirt* or any title. ABFE believes the entire community of the book is strengthened when, together, we reaffirm the right of booksellers to curate their stores and to schedule events as they see fit, in light of their communities and the staff.

Critical examination of fiction and nonfiction work is welcome, as is protest and counter speech. Reasoned and robust debate on any published work makes our nation and our culture more diverse and stronger.

IN THIS ESSAY, I've devoted a fair amount of time and ink to parsing some distinctions that I think have been obscured in many debates about free expression. These distinctions matter, I believe, because they can help those of us who work in the publishing chain to think more clearly about the business decisions we make.

We shouldn't be afraid of allowing our personal values to influence our choices about which books to publish, distribute, or promote—because, whether we realize it or not, we express our personal values in every such choice we make. Our goal should be to do so consciously, deliberately, and thoughtfully, so that the books we publish can express our own best values and those of the kind of society we'd like to live in.

We shouldn't fall into the error of assuming that a "value-neutral" or "apolitical" philosophy is the best or only one for a publisher or bookseller to adopt. Some publishers may decide they want to publish the widest possible range of books, from those on the far right to those on the far left—and that's a perfectly valid approach. But others may choose a politically engaged posture and choose to publish books that promote a specific political or social perspective—and that's perfectly valid, too.

Similarly, a particular bookstore may be happy to make space on its shelves for books that include far-right, white nationalist tomes as well as radical leftist or anarchist volumes—and may even choose to host book events for the corresponding groups of readers. God bless them (and protect them)! But a different bookstore may choose a much more narrowly focused approach to stock selection and community outreach—one that is strongly feminist, or evangelical, or LGBTQ-oriented, or socially and politically conservative. I wish them all success. And in a country as vast, varied, and dynamic as the United States, there's surely room for them all. Which means that not every bookstore is required to display *The Turner Diaries* on its shelves—nor *The 1619 Project*. And if a particular store freely chooses not to do so, then "censorship" is not involved.

Finally, we shouldn't confuse criticism of a book—even harsh, angry, unfair criticism—with censorship. Readers desperately want the world to acknowledge the validity of their ideas, the values of their identities, and the dignity of their life stories—all of which means they want to see books published that capture and reflect those truths. So they care passionately about books—thank God. And as a result of those passions, when heated battles over the content of particular books arise, there will be times when tempers flare and people say and do things that are intemperate. That's okay, too. Civility is an important value. It's not all-important, nor is it the single most important value in a free society.

In the end, freedom itself—messy, contentious, irascible, painful freedom—is the value we need to cherish and protect. If we keep our eyes on that prize, we won't go far wrong.

POSTSCRIPT: As I conclude this essay, I wonder what Joyce Meskis would think about my arguments. I suspect she'd agree with some and want to knock down others—likely with a pointed question or a well-chosen counter-example. I don't know for sure. But one thing I do know is that I wish Joyce was still here to take part in the conversation! As she always did, she would make our world of books and publishing a smarter, better place.—K.W.

16.
Books Unbanned

Nick Higgins and Amy Mikel

Nick Higgins and Amy Mikel of the Brooklyn Public Library are two members of the team that, in 2022, created the Books Unbanned program, which provides free ebook access to teens and young adults nationwide, in defiance of rising book challenges across the country. For their efforts, the Books Unbanned team were named Librarians of the Year by Library Journal, *the nation's leading publication for librarians.*

B ROOKLYN PUBLIC LIBRARY (BPL) stands firmly against censorship and for the principle of intellectual freedom—the right of every individual to seek and receive information from all points of view without restriction. We believe limited or one-sided information is a threat to democracy itself.

Challenges to books and ideas have always been a part of the library landscape, but recent efforts have become far more coordinated and effective, requiring libraries, schools, First Amendment advocates, community members, publishers, booksellers, parents, and others to become equally well-coordinated and to fight back with collective purpose.

Books Unbanned is BPL's freedom-to-read campaign that gives any teen in the country experiencing local book bans or other challenges free access to our entire digital book collection. It grew from a brief conversation between two colleagues early in 2022 who were discussing book bans that were proliferating across several states, including Texas. It has since grown into a national intellectual freedom network of organizations, advocates, teens, and libraries.

Like other librarians, we at BPL are expert at drawing attention to censorship threats and showcasing writers who are commonly targets of book bans. We felt that the recent pattern of book bans and challenges represented something different from what we've seen in some time, and required a response more impactful than creating banned book displays or reading groups.

In November 2021, Matt Krause—a state representative in Texas—pulled together a list of 850 books that he and his staff determined to be inappropriate for kids. He demanded that the Texas Education Agency identify how many copies of each book were in which schools in his district and how much they cost. He also asked the agency to surface other books in those schools that touch on topics including ". . . human sexuality, sexually transmitted diseases, or human immunodeficiency virus (HIV) or acquired immune deficiency syndrome (AIDS), sexually explicit images, graphic presentations of sexual behavior that is in violation of the law, or contain material that might make students feel discomfort, guilt, anguish, or any other form of psychological distress because of their race or sex or convey that a student, by virtue of their race or sex, is inherently racist, sexist, or oppressive, whether consciously or unconsciously."

Krause's extraordinarily sweeping order and the accompanying book list came out as more and more stories were emerging of usually staid school board meetings being turned upside down by known extremist and white supremacist groups like the Proud Boys and Moms for Liberty. Reports by the American Library Association and PEN America showed that book bans and challenges were increasing at an alarming rate in communities across the country, and that demands for the removal of race- and gender-specific books were becoming more virulent and public. Teachers and librarians were being criminalized by the state for essentially doing the jobs they were trained, and hired, to do. Many were absorbing vicious harassment online and across the reference desk.

These censorship efforts—in part a continuation of Covid-era grievances born from resentment of masking and vaccine mandates, racial justice initiatives, stay-at-home orders, and other perceived harms—were largely fueled by sophisticated national networking and communications strategies deployed by those extremist groups, and also by attempts by elected state officials to "win the culture wars" by flooding legislatures with educational gag orders.

Book challenges and bans are not a new phenomenon in libraries. But what struck us as different about Krause's list is that it signaled a brazen marshaling of state power to effectively remove books from schools and classrooms, at the same time delegitimizing the existence of certain communities while granting the state's imprimatur to others. Books were being used as a vehicle to get to the larger, darker goal of marginalizing and even criminalizing entire groups of people in society—people of color and LGBTQ+ communities specifically.

This kind of gross overreach of state power and bigotry is familiar. Throughout history, there have been similar examples of authoritarianism and state-sponsored white supremacism rising out of fear and backlash to pluralism. Yet in those moments in history, there have been abundant examples of righteous individuals, institutions, and whole communities motivated to collective action in resistance to such assaults. Our hope is that the present moment will call forth a similar response.

Our responsibility as library professionals is to ensure everyone can freely exercise their right to read whatever they want and to both seek and receive information from all points of view without restriction. This drives the majority of our work in public libraries and informs all of our decisions, leading to the range of diverse points of view and topics you can find on the library shelves. Book selection is done by professional librarians to ensure that the widest and deepest spectrum of ideas and subjects possible is available to all.

Intellectual freedom also requires mechanisms for members of the reading public to challenge or object to what we have chosen to put on the shelves. You may find a book in our collection that you think shouldn't be there, and it is your right to talk to us about it and challenge its merit. Access to robust discourse on what is or is not reflective of our community's values is also an essential right that we practice and defend.

Libraries and schools should have a well-written and understandable policy that details the process a member of the public can take in order to challenge a book. For us in Brooklyn, and in many other libraries and schools, this means providing a readily available form that any member of the public can use to write about a book they object to and why they think it should be removed from the library. People who object to a particular title must confirm that they have read the book from cover to cover—a bedrock requirement for any good-faith debate on a book's merits or lack thereof. At BPL, we have a committee of librarians who review the requests for reconsideration of materials and will read the books being challenged cover to cover, debate their merits, and interrogate the challenge as written. Following those deliberations, the committee submits a recommendation to the Chief Librarian, who will then decide to either reject the challenge or position it for debate with the Board of Trustees. Throughout the process, each step and decision is communicated back to the person who challenged the book in the first place.

This commitment to intellectual freedom is not new to libraries. In the late 1930s, during the run-up to World War II and the rise of totalitarian regimes in Europe, a number of book-banning cases were sprouting up across the United States, with books like John Steinbeck's *The Grapes of Wrath* being pulled from shelves. In response, a Library Bill of Rights was drafted by library director Forrest Spaulding from Des Moines, Iowa, to speak out against the "growing intolerance, suppression of free speech and censorship affecting the rights of minorities and individuals." It became a foundational document in support of free expression.

In the 1950s, another threat to intellectual freedom was emerging as the Red Scare engulfed American politics and public discourse. Grassroots anti-communist groups took root in towns all over the country. Members of these groups antagonized educators and librarians in attempts to force libraries and schools to remove books that they felt were sympathetic to communist causes, anti-American, or otherwise inappropriate for an American reading public.

This spate of book challenges and bans prompted a group of librarians and publishers to work with the American Library Association to build upon the Library Bill of Rights and create a Freedom to Read Statement. While the Library Bill of Rights centered largely on the rights of library users to read books and to use spaces as they see fit, the Freedom to Read Statement was unambiguous in its focus on the *responsibilities* that librarians and publishers have in pushing back on all attempts at censorship wherever it is found, in whatever form it comes. It begins:

We believe that free communication is essential to the preservation of a free society and a creative culture. We believe that these pressures toward conformity present the danger of limiting the range and variety of inquiry and expression on which our democracy and our culture depend. We believe that every

American community must jealously guard the freedom to publish and to circulate, in order to preserve its own freedom to read. We believe that publishers and librarians have a profound responsibility to give validity to that freedom to read by making it possible for the readers to choose freely from a variety of offerings.

The freedom to read is guaranteed by the Constitution. Those with faith in free people will stand firm on these constitutional guarantees of essential rights and will exercise the responsibilities that accompany these rights.

Today, a new wave of threats to free expression is under way. In response, In response, during National Library Week in April 2022, we launched Books Unbanned. We aimed to support young adults across the United States who were facing bans and challenges to books in their local school or public libraries. Our hope was to position BPL as a champion of intellectual freedom at home and anywhere in the country where it was being challenged. We developed three goals for the program that continue to drive our work today.

Goal 1: Offer direct support to teens, no matter where they live

Through Books Unbanned, BPL gives free, out-of-state eCards to any young adult in the United States, allowing them access to the over 500,000 eBooks and audio books in our collection (along with a broad range of databases). All they need to do is send us a note asking for the card and telling us a bit about the access or censorship issues they may be facing. As of June 2023, BPL has issued over 6,500 new young adult eCards to individuals in all 50 states, Washington, DC, and Puerto Rico.

Stated this way, the scope of the project may sound straightforward, even obvious. In reality, it wasn't so simple.

In our early internal conversations about what would eventually become Books Unbanned, we tried to think of ways we could both push back and take a stand while also directly supporting the people who were being impacted by the Krause list—students, librarians, teachers, and community members. We came up with the idea of giving every person in Krause's district a free Brooklyn Public Library card, handing them unrestricted, free access to our entire digital collection. This earliest written pitch reflects the simplicity of the action that has carried through to how the program operates today:

For the month of February, we propose waiving our $50 out-of-state eCard fee for young adults, age 13 to 21, residing in the district of Texas state representative Matt Krause. The card will be in good standing for a year. Krause, chairman of the Texas House of Representatives General Investigating Committee, has called for public school libraries to search their collections for 850 "sexually explicit or racially preferential books." Teens in Llano County—where books have already been removed from the public library shelves—will also be eligible to participate. Texas residents can also request a free eCard to access the digital collections of Houston Public Library and Harris County Public Library (and other TX libraries), which we will promote in all of our communications. Though many young adults in these areas may not take advantage of the expanded access to BPL (or Texas Library) eBook collections, we hope to center libraries as leaders in advancing and defending foundational democratic values.

Costs associated with this intervention include:

- o Revenue loss from any new eCards created for this group of Texas residents through the month of February.
- o Purchasing of new eBook licenses to offset any strain on our catalog holdings (and Brooklyn card users) due to increased check-outs from this group.
- o Funding to set three or four eBook titles from the "banned book list" to always available status. We would keep those titles perpetually available so no patron (in Brooklyn or Texas) would ever have to wait to check them out.

But it turned out that having librarians from Brooklyn go down to Texas to pick a fight would have actually been a really bad idea. We checked in with our friends in the Texas Library Association (TLA), offering our solidarity and support. The good people at the TLA informed us that our initial idea, though kind-hearted, would place too bright a spotlight on some of the libraries currently struggling in the crosshairs of an intensifying culture war. They were right, of course—and extremely kind in their rejection of our misguided offer.

In retrospect, our thinking was embryonic, naïve, too reactive to the urgency of the crisis, and not thoughtful enough in addressing the larger, more pernicious threats. Still, we knew there was something there worth following up on.

Even before we reached out to our friends in Texas, there had been a fair amount of skepticism expressed internally here at the library. Perhaps it wasn't legal to provide local resources across state lines. Perhaps the focus on offering digital services to people out of state would (at best) distract attention from or(at worst) exacerbate the significant digital divide experienced by some of our most vulnerable communities at home. Maybe this just wasn't a good use of internal staff time and resources. It could be seen as a cynical way to get attention, without offering any truly transformative interventions for people. There might not be a lot of interest in the campaign, and it could land with a thud.

Maybe we wouldn't be able to fundraise for it, and there could be backlash from our own constituents, who might see this as siphoning off resources from our own communities here in Brooklyn. Maybe this is just a gimmick.

These concerns were brought up often in the early going when the idea was just learning how to crawl. The concerns about the purpose, impact, and values of the initiative helped focus energy and attention on the development of goals and why this, above all other things, deserved to be front and center as an expression of who we are as an institution.

Getting the polite decline from Texas caused us to rethink the audience. The head of our external affairs department asked whether we could broaden our range and offer the card to any young adult anywhere in the country. That way, we wouldn't be picking a fight with any particular state or group but would instead be fighting the battle against censorship and in favor of First Amendment rights more broadly and concretely. The revised plan that we ultimately put into effect does just that.

Goal 2: Center teens in everything we do— nothing for teens without teens

For us at Brooklyn Public Library, the current highly coordinated and focused effort is to ban books is not just about books. It's about erasing the experiences and voices of actual human beings. Libraries are often considered neutral spaces and librarianship a neutral profession, but we are not neutral when it comes to censorship and our responsibility to push back against efforts to silence people in our communities. So many of the record number of books challenged and banned in 2021 relate to LGBTQ+ topics and feature people of color in their narratives or are written by Black or LGBTQ+ authors. The removal of these stories and experiences from the shelves of a library will immediately signal to a young person of color or to LGBTQ teens that not only do their experiences not matter, but that any evidence of their existence has no place in the community. So our work at its most basic level is about making sure that kids have the right to live their lives without persecution or fear.

The way we've managed the program reflects the importance of centering young people. Not only did a group of teens from Brooklyn (a core group of some of our interns here at the library) come up with the name Books Unbanned, they also established a national Teen Intellectual Freedom Council. The monthly, teen-led virtual sessions of this council give teens an opportunity to learn about censorship issues their peers are facing in other parts of the country, access resources that can help in pushing back against local challenges and bans, and to learn about freedom-to-read issues in greater depth from guest speakers and advocates. The library sends a special welcome letter to all new teen cardholders, reaffirming our commitment to the freedom to read whatever you want to read, sharing resources like our BookMatch Teen readers' advisory service, and extending an invitation to join our Teen Intellectual Freedom Council meetings. The new teen cardholders from across the country are tuning in to council meetings to discuss what they are seeing on the ground in their own communities, the strategies they are using to push back on censorship efforts, and importantly, creating with one another a network of support and allyship that has the potential to evolve beyond issues of intellectual freedom. We think these young people will emerge as cohorts of thoughtful leaders across multiple sectors in a more hopeful future.

Books Unbanned has been a successful library program. The eCards for young people are being issued in large numbers in states that are experiencing the most concentrated efforts to ban books, including Texas, Tennessee, Florida, and Oklahoma. States like Vermont, Maine, and Oregon are also strong adopters of Books Unbanned, where the cards are used to address book access challenges in largely rural areas with less immediate physical access to a well-resourced public library.

With their cards, these new members of the BPL community are checking out an average of 8,000 eBooks and audiobooks per month. The campaign has generated around two million impressions with social media engagement and around 2.6 billion impressions with earned media. In addition to the tens of thousands of emails we've received from teens looking to sign up for a BPL library card, we've also heard from teachers, parents, librarians, and community members—people from all backgrounds and experiences who champion the program not necessarily because they love libraries (though those fine folks are certainly in the majority), but because they see in the effort an expression of the values they share for a pluralistic, inclusive, and compassionate society. For many of the writers who contact us, the program reflects their principled aspirations for their families and communities.

Goal 3: Take back the narrative

A third goal of Books Unbanned is to amplify our message about intellectual freedom and healthy engagement in civil society. Coverage of book bans and challenges is often driven by those who are demanding that books be pulled from classrooms and library shelves. Their voices are often loud and provocative and receive wide attention. Libraries have an opportunity to steer the narrative around the principle of intellectual freedom and the critical role it plays in libraries and a democratic society. Our Books Unbanned project, like so many other teen-led initiatives that have sprung up across the United States to push back against censorship, aims to keep the stories and experiences of all members of our communities in the public discourse—especially the stories and experiences of those who find themselves at the business end of these attacks.

This is a narrative that resonates with people who are currently library supporters, and importantly, those who haven't been in a library in years. We have received thousands of messages from people who love what we're doing, but may not fully know what a library does.

What we seek are ways to tell compelling stories about our libraries—stories about what the library means to the communities we serve, our place in our society, and the value we give now and long into the future. Many of us who grew up in libraries and caught the bug early on are tuned into what makes the library so great, so welcoming, and so inspiring. Many people feel that way about libraries. In poll after poll on the trustworthiness of public institutions, libraries rank consistently near the top of the list. We are a profession that enjoys a ton of inherited good will, and our job in most cases is to make good on it and to keep it going by creating new ways for people to find a home here long into the future.

In these days of political polarization and government budget cuts, the very survival of libraries is dependent on how well we tell those stories to the already converted—all of those reading this book, our regular patrons and supporters who year over year go to bat for the library, and so many more. But it is even more critical for us to find out how to tell the story of the library so that it resonates with people who might not have stepped foot in a library since childhood—or ever. We need to go well beyond the walls of the library and connect with people who are looking for representations of how they think society should be organized, how communities should be built, and how people should take care of one another. In short, ours is a story about how we aspire to live with one another with the time we have.

What we've found with Books Unbanned is that it helps to tell a cogent, urgent story about how we want to live with one another as a society, and what we stand to lose if that vision is destroyed. Of the thousands of emails and text messages we've received since the beginning of the campaign, many are from parents, caregivers, and adult community members who simply want to know how they can get involved in standing up for intellectual freedom and pushing against the rise of authoritarianism.

It is unusual that public libraries exist in 2024 America. They are by many measures good expressions of our democratic values at a time when those types of examples are becoming increasingly rare. Libraries are places that are available and welcoming to everyone in the community. There are no restrictions on access. It doesn't matter your age, ability, background, race, education, financial standing, citizenship, or anything else: Come as you are, and take what you want. Libraries are held together by a social contract—an agreement that everyone be included, everyone be given equal access to everything they find there, from the books on the shelves and the programs they attend to the spaces that they sit in. People have a responsibility to take care of the things they find in the library—the books as well as the other people in the space. We are a decidedly non-commercial space. We value civic engagement, free expression, and community building.

Thus, in so many ways, libraries are expressions of what our democracy aspires to be. And if there were no system of public libraries in this country today and we tried to build them from scratch, it would take a miracle to get them off the ground.

It is hard to believe we're having this discussion in 2024, but here we are. Over the course of history, there has always been a small, but loud, minority of voices who are afraid of difference, afraid of having their ideas challenged, afraid of having their biases and dark bigotry exposed. Many will wrap themselves up in innocuous sounding campaigns espousing "liberty" or "parental rights" or "family values." These are always the adults at the front of the line at a council hearing or a school board meeting, demanding that their kids not be exposed to one thing or another in the library or classroom, demanding that certain books be pulled from the shelves and hidden away.

Healthy democracies—thriving societies—require the fostering of connections among people with different points of view, understanding among people of different backgrounds and experiences, on-going dialog and debate, inclusion, and participation of everyone. Imagine being a teen and walking into a place that is supposed to contain the widest spectrum of human ideas, experiences, and identities, and instead finding out that (even here in the library!), you don't belong.

At Brooklyn Public Library, we stand with any individual or organization who stands for intellectual freedom and against censorship. We are proud to work with Seattle Public Library, which launched its own version of Books Unbanned in April 2023 and issued nearly 3,000 eCards to kids all over the United States in a short two months. We support the Los Angeles County Public Library, which planned a California Books Unbanned initiative for October 2023. We will continue to partner with PEN America on hosting virtual Freedom to Read Institutes for teens across the country.

Most important, we stand in solidarity with the countless educators, students, parents, booksellers, publishers, writers, and community members who are committed to defending and expanding the right to read.

Acknowledgments

ASSEMBLING THIS BOOK—a collection of insights and stories about the industry to which I've devoted my working life, produced in tribute to one of the publishing heroes I admire most—has been a labor of love and a joy for me. It would not have been possible without the support and friendship of the three people closest to Joyce Meskis: her husband Jed and her daughters Katherine and Julie. Thanks to them for their help, advice, and enthusiasm. The time I spent with them on this project is an additional gift that I've cherished.

I'm also deeply grateful to the distinguished professionals who gave of their time and talent to contribute chapters to the book: Betsy Burton, David Emblidge, Chris Finan, David R. Godine, U.S. Senator John Hickenlooper, Nick Higgins, Carole Horne, Richard Howorth, Jack Jensen, Carl Lennertz, Amy Mikel, Matthew Miller, Chuck Robinson, Jill Smith, Clara Villarosa (and her daughter Linda Villarosa), and Steve Zansberg. I learned so much from the opportunity to work with these leaders of the book world, and I know that many readers will appreciate the chance to benefit from their wisdom as well.

Finally, a word about the professionals at Arc Indexing, who prepare the indexes for Rivertowns Books. They joined the chapter authors in offering to provide their services *pro bono* to help support the American Library Association Office for Intellectual Freedom, which will receive all proceeds from this book. My thanks for their generosity.

K.W.

Index

About Joyce Meskis

J OYCE MESKIS WAS BORN in East Chicago, Indiana in 1942. As a young girl, she spent much of her time in libraries and remembered carrying stacks of books home and being read bedtime stories by her mother.

Her love of books continued into her adult life. She worked in libraries and bookstores to help pay for her college tuition at Purdue University. After earning a degree in English, she moved to Littleton, Colorado with her first husband and began raising a family.

Not long after moving to Colorado she realized her calling in life. A few years later, now divorced, she decided to open her own bookstore in Parker, Colorado. Later, in 1974, Joyce purchased a small store in the Cherry Creek neighborhood of Denver called the Tattered Cover Book Store, which she grew into one of the largest bookstores in the nation.

Joyce's passion was putting books and people together, and providing a comfortable place where people could browse a vast selection of ideas in print. She received recognition and many accolades as owner of a successful independent bookstore and for her work in support of free speech and the First Amendment. Yet for Joyce, success was ensuring that the freedom to read is guaranteed and that books of all varieties and viewpoints are accessible to everyone. As a bookseller, Joyce believed being an advocate for readers and supporting a marketplace of ideas were paramount responsibilities.

Joyce was known to most as a bookstore owner, but what few people knew about was her passion for cooking. She had bookshelves full of cookbooks with many handwritten notes alongside her favorite recipes. She especially loved cooking traditional Lithuanian food and having large meals with family and friends. She would often start planning the menu weeks ahead and took the time and care to make each gathering memorable for everyone.

Thanksgiving with Joyce and her husband Jed was often a huge event with family and friends from across the country gathering for a traditional feast. Joyce and Jed loved to travel and they took many trips, including several to Lithuania to visit Joyce's extended family. She was very interested in researching her Lithuanian heritage as both her maternal and paternal grandparents immigrated from there.

Most of all Joyce cherished time spent with her children, her grandchildren, and Jed, the love of her life.

About the Editor

K ARL WEBER, publisher of Rivertowns Books, is a writer, editor, and book developer with over forty years' experience in the book publishing industry. He is an expert in general-interest nonfiction publishing, specializing in topics from business and personal finance to politics, current affairs, history, autobiography, self-help, and personal development.

Weber has advised and assisted authors in a wide range of nonfiction areas, including, for example, former president Jimmy Carter, author of several *New York Times* bestsellers, including *An Hour Before Daylight* (2000), which Weber edited; Muhammad Yunus, winner of the 2006 Nobel Peace Prize, with whom Weber co-authored the *New York Times* bestseller *Creating a World Without Poverty* (2008) and its sequels, *Building Social Business* (2010) and *A World of Three Zeros* (2017); and the late Ash Carter, secretary of defense under Barack Obama, whose book *Inside the Five-Sided Box* (2019) Weber edited.

Before founding Rivertowns Books, Weber served as managing director of the Times Business imprint at Random House (1994-1997) and as senior editor and publisher in the trade book division of John Wiley & Sons (1986-1994). Weber is director of the Editing Workshop at the Denver Publishing Institute, a summer program for individuals interested in pursuing or advancing careers in the publishing industry.

Weber lives in Irvington, New York, with his wife, Mary-Jo Weber.

Printed in the USA
CPSIA information can be obtained
at www.ICGtesting.com
LVHW040743100424
776895LV00007B/36